Aussie

STEM Stars

CRESWELL EASTMAN

The man who saved a million brains

Aussie STEM Stars

CRESWELL EASTMAN

The man who saved a million brains

Story told by PENNY TANGEY

Aussie STEM Stars series
Published by Wild Dingo Press
Melbourne, Australia
books@wilddingopress.com.au
wilddingopress.com.au

This work was first published by Wild Dingo Press 2022

Cover Design: Gisela Beer
Illustrations: Mirjana Segan
Series Editor: Catherine Lewis
Printed in Australia.

Tangey, Penny 1981-, author.
Creswell Eastman: The man who saved a million brains/Penny Tangey

A catalogue record for this book is available from the National Library of Australia

ISBN: 9781925893526 (paperback)
ISBN: 9781925893533 (epdf)
ISBN: 9781925893540 (Epub)

Never see problems as too large and difficult;
always break them down.
– Creswell Eastman

Disclaimer

This work has been developed in collaboration with Professor Creswell Eastman. The utmost care has been taken to respectfully portray, as accurately as memory allows, the events and the stories of all who appear in this work. The publishers assume no liability or responsibility for unintended inaccuracies but would be pleased to rectify at the earliest opportunity any omissions or errors brought to their notice.

Contents

1

The fighting nun

Cres dipped his pen into the inkwell on his desk. He quickly and neatly copied the problem on the blackboard into his exercise book. The other kids were working on different sums, but his teacher, Sister Patrick, had set a problem just for him. It was about an aeroplane because she knew Cres loved anything to do with planes.

The room was silent except for the scratching of pen nibs on paper. The classroom door squeaked open, but Cres didn't look up. He was too absorbed in calculating how much fuel a plane needed to fly around the world.

Sister Patrick's voice said, 'Creswell Eastman, please go with Sister Francis.'

Cres looked up to see the Senior School teacher standing in the doorway. Like all the teachers at St Joseph's, Sister Francis wore a floor-length brown robe, called a habit, with a brown veil covering her head. Her face was encircled with white material, which also covered her neck and most of her forehead. Only her face and hands were visible. Wooden beads and a cross hung from her waist.

Cres slid out of his seat. His deskmate, Jack, looked quizzically at him. Cres shrugged—he had no idea what Sister Francis wanted.

He followed her along the school's main corridor, walking past students' bags hanging on hooks along the wall.

St Joseph's was a small school, teaching students aged 5 to 15. After that, most kids left school and got a job. Many nuns who taught there hadn't been educated past primary school themselves, but they tried hard to give the local Catholic kids a good start.

The nuns were officially called **Sisters of St Joseph's of the Sacred Heart**, but they were usually called Brown Joeys because of their brown habits. They devoted their lives to God, lived together in a convent, and were teachers during the day. The kids loved to imagine what the nuns did in the convent. Cres's mother said they prayed and did good works, but there were more exciting rumours.

Mary McKillop founded the **Sisters of St Joseph's of the Sacred Heart** in Australia in 1866. The nuns ran children's homes and Catholic schools in New South Wales. In 2010 the Catholic Church recognised Mary MacKillop as Australia's first saint.

Sister Francis led Cres towards the senior school classroom. From the corridor Cres heard loud shouts and talking. When she opened the door the noise changed to scrambling and scraping as the students hurried to their desks.

Cres noted the room's similarities to the junior classroom. Two rows of wooden desks, with attached benches seated two students at each desk. A different smell hung in the air, sharp like eucalyptus leaves but unpleasant. Cres's eye was drawn to the posters on the wall. He recognised the periodic table of chemical elements. He couldn't wait to study things like that.

In the second row sat Cres's sister, Margaret, who looked surprised to see him.

'We have a special guest today,' Sister Francis said. 'This is Creswell Eastman from the junior class. He's a very clever boy and today you will practise your arithmetic against him.'

He smiled when she handed him a piece of chalk. He liked maths races—this would be fun.

One by one the students came to the front to solve maths problems against Cres.

Cres wasn't trying to show off, he just wrote the answers as fast as he could, which turned out to be faster than anyone else.

His sister was last. Cres knew she was good with numbers. This would be a challenge.

Sister Francis said, '206 times 14'.

Margaret and Cres wrote furiously. In her hurry, Margaret's chalk snapped in half. She lost a precious second and Cres managed to write 2,884 before his sister did.

He'd beaten the entire class!

'Can you believe Cres is only nine years old! We are lucky to have such a clever boy at St Joseph's,' Sister Francis beamed. 'Please give him a round of applause.'

The students scowled and clapped unenthusiastically. Cres's happiness changed to nervousness. The chalky dust mixed with the sweat on his hands forming a paste. He caught Margaret's eye and she gave him a half smile. He couldn't tell if she was proud of him, or embarrassed.

Standing in a room full of high school students, he felt separate and alone.

He walked back to his classroom and slid into his seat next to Jack. They exchanged glances, but Sister Patrick demanded strict silence, so Cres couldn't explain. He continued working on his aeroplane problem, but he couldn't enjoy it, remembering the dirty looks from the older kids.

At the end of the day the school bell clanged. Cres grabbed his bag from the hook in the corridor and walked to the bus stop. Passing the tank stand, someone called out.

'Hey, Creswell!'

Cres turned and saw an older boy, who he recognised from Margaret's class.

'Hi,' said Cres, smiling.

The boy came up and pushed him in the chest. Cres stumbled and fell backwards heavily onto a bench, banging the back of his legs. They were hidden behind the tank stand. No one could see what was happening.

The older boy towered over him and asked, 'What's 49 squared?'

'2401.'

It was the right answer, but the boy punched him anyway, before walking off.

In a daze, Cres stumbled up and continued to the bus stop. He felt a trickle on his face and touched his chin. There was blood on his fingers. He got out his handkerchief and pressed it to his face.

Margaret was already waiting at the bus stop.

'What happened?'

'You know,' said Cres, 'the usual.' Margaret had seen older boys pushing Cres around before. She stuck up for him when she could.

'Here,' said Margaret, handing him a clean handkerchief, embroidered with pink roses.

He shoved his bloodied handkerchief in his pocket and held the clean one to his face.

With relief Cres saw the familiar bus approaching with its blue and white waves painted on the side and the words: 'Evans Head—Woodburn'.

Stepping onto the bus, he greeted the driver.

'You won't bleed on my seats, will you?' said the driver gruffly.

Cres shook his head.

'Boys! Always getting into fights.'

Cres hadn't wanted to be in a fight. He wasn't even sure he had been.

Finding an empty seat, he slumped into it, glad to be leaving Woodburn and going home.

Someone sat heavily in the seat beside him. Cres feared the older boy had followed him, then realised with relief, that it was only Jack.

'How do you think Australia will go in South Africa without Bradman?' his friend asked.

Bradman had been Australia's champion test cricketer for twenty years and had retired recently with a test batting average agonisingly close to 100.

Jack didn't seem to notice Cres was bleeding, so Cres ignored it too.

'I think Hassett'll do well.' His voice sounded shaky, but cricket talk was a good distraction for the 20-minute bus ride home.

In Evans Head, Margaret and Cres walked from the bus stop to their house where Cres's brown retriever greeted them at the gate.

'Hello, Princey!' Cres exclaimed happily.

Margaret gave Prince a quick pat, then headed inside. Cres suspected she'd tell his eldest sister Barbara what had happened at school. Margaret always wanted to be first with any news.

Cres stayed outside with Prince for a few minutes.

'How are you, boy? Do you want to come fishing on the weekend? Catch fish?'

Prince wagged his tail even harder. If dogs ever flew, this is how it would start, he reckoned.

'Not today, boy. On the weekend.' Dogs didn't understand the past or future; right now, was everything to them.

Cres went inside and found Barbara standing at the kitchen sink washing up.

'Hi,' he said. 'Where's Mum?'

'In the bedroom. Dad's home from work. He's not feeling well.' Barbara turned to him. 'Marg said you got hurt?'

Cres nodded. He took away the handkerchief to show her.

Barbara winced when she saw his face. She shook her head. 'The teachers should look after you better.'

'I can look after myself,' Cres said.

'I'm sure you can,' Barbara responded. 'Just have a seat there.' She pointed at a bright blue kitchen chair painted to match the kitchen bench tops and the linoleum floor.

Barbara was training to be a nurse, so Cres supposed fixing up his injuries was good practise.

She examined his face. 'Well, the bleeding's stopped. I'll just clean it up.'

She left the room, returning with a wet flannel and a tub of ointment called **Iodex**. Cres's mother always kept some in the house and believed the ointment could cure any skin complaint including bruises, grazes and rashes.

Most Australian families had **Iodex** in their medicine cupboard in the 1950s and 60s. It is an antiseptic cream that contains iodine, an element that would play a big role in Cres's discoveries.

First, Barbara cleaned the cut with the flannel. It stung, but Cres tried not to move. Then she dabbed the brown ointment onto the cut under his lip.

Margaret came back and stood in the kitchen doorway watching.

'I think this should heal up nicely,' said Barbara reassuringly.

'Well, he has fat lips anyway. No one will notice,' Margaret said with a smirk.

'Hey!' Cres said, jumping off his chair. Margaret always teased him, and he always reacted. 'I'll give you a fat lip!' he yelled.

Margaret laughed as she walked away. She knew Cres would never hurt her. He hated violence.

Cres went to follow her, but Barbara put a hand on his shoulder. 'Hey, I'm not finished with you, yet.'

He sat back down while his sister got him a piece of bread with jam. He ate a few bites, chewing on the good side of his mouth but he didn't feel hungry. Thinking about going to school and facing the older kids again turned his stomach. He couldn't understand why the kids were mad at him. He hadn't asked to be good at maths, and he hadn't wanted to show off. Sister Francis had made him do it. Now the other kids hated him. It wasn't fair.

*

The next day when the lunchtime bell rang Cres lifted the lid of his desk and put his books away neatly. Standing up was a relief. The hard, wooden seat was painful with the bruises on his legs.

He jostled towards the classroom door with the others, planning to stay in a group so the older boy wouldn't corner him alone again.

'Creswell Eastman! Stay back, please,' called Sister Patrick.

He sighed. What now? He shuffled towards the blackboard and waited while the other kids went out.

Sister Patrick shut the door and stood in front of him. The normally cheerful nun looked disapproving.

'Creswell Eastman,' she said, 'look at the state of you'.

He brought his hand to his face, which was sore and swollen.

'I tripped on a step,' he said quickly. That's what he'd told his mother and she'd believed him. Luckily, his sisters hadn't told her the truth.

Sister Patrick raised her eyebrows. 'What are we going to do with you?'

Cres wasn't sure. He hoped Sister Patrick wouldn't tell his mother. Disappointing nuns was on her list of top worst things a son could do, just behind disappointing priests.

'You need to learn how to fight back,' she said.

'Pardon?' Cres was sure she'd tell him off for fighting, not encourage him.

'You need to defend yourself. And I can teach you.'

Cres was surprised and doubtful. It wasn't just the nun's clothes, although the brown habit didn't scream 'fighter'. Sister Patrick was also tiny, only a little taller than him. The older kids at St Joseph's already loomed above her.

Nevertheless, there she was, standing in front of him with her fists up.

'Hit me,' she commanded.

'Pardon?'

'Hit me!'

Cres usually obeyed his teachers, but he stared at Sister Patrick unmoving. He couldn't hit her.

Firstly, she was his teacher, and it must be against the school rules to hit a teacher.

Secondly, his parents taught him to look after people. Hitting someone was the opposite.

Thirdly, she was a nun. Nuns were women. That meant they had bosoms. Cres had heard of breast cancer and knew it was a serious illness that women could die from. If you punched a woman in the bosom, it might cause cancer. That's what he'd heard.

If he punched Sister Patrick, he could kill her. Then what would his mother say? Killing a nun was way worse than disappointing one.

'Creswell Eastman, hit me this instant!' said Sister Patrick, raising her voice.

'What if I hurt you?'

'Good luck to you! Now hit me!'

Reluctantly, Cres jabbed his fist at her. Sister Patrick neatly ducked to the side avoiding his punch.

'Do you see what I did there?' she asked.

She threw a punch at Cres, landing it on his shoulder. He staggered, shocked by the force of the little nun's fist.

Over lunchtime, Sister Patrick demonstrated basic boxing techniques, how to avoid punches and throw them back. Cres never came close to landing a blow on his teacher—he was too scared, and she was too quick—but she seemed pleased with his progress anyway.

'You're a fast learner,' she said, dabbing her face with a large handkerchief produced from the depths of her robes.

Cres shrugged. It was probably true, but he didn't think about it. His mother had taught him to read before he started school, so he'd always been ahead. At least, it made schoolwork easier.

After school, Cres walked towards the bus stop, clammy with nervous sweat, feeling as if he might throw up. He didn't want to fight. He didn't want to be hurt and he didn't want to hurt other people. He wished he was brave like his dad. Albert Eastman had fought in World War I and although he didn't talk about it often, he'd faced things Cres couldn't imagine.

The boy was waiting for Cres at the tank stand again. Cres's stomach dropped. The boy stepped towards him and threw a punch but Cres managed to duck away. He approached again. This time Cres swung a fist and connected with the boy's stomach, causing him to double over in pain.

'Are you okay?' Cres asked, his hand throbbing.

The boy straightened up with fury in his eyes. Cres turned and ran to the safety of the bus stop.

He'd stood up for himself, but he wished he didn't have to. He was a fast learner, but it was hard to know if that was a good thing yet.

2

Fishing

On Saturday, the day stretched ahead of Cres, free of school, nuns, and boxing lessons. He stood on the verandah looking across an empty paddock to his favourite view, the Evans Head aerodrome, which had been a Royal Australian Air Force training base during World War II. It was the reason the Eastmans had moved here because Cres's dad worked on communication systems at the base.

Sometimes Cres's dad smuggled him into the aerodrome under a rug on the car's back seat. It was exhilarating going through the checkpoints, trying to lie still under the hot and prickly fabric.

Once they were in, Cres loved watching the planes and hearing their engines roar up close.

There was a housing shortage during the war, so when the Eastmans first moved to Evans Head they lived in a tent fitted out with furniture. Cres's mother, Meg, hadn't complained because others suffered more in wartime. Anyway, soon more houses were built and the Eastmans moved into one.

Meg liked the new house because the walls didn't move and dirt didn't blow in with the wind.

Cres liked it because he could watch planes from the verandah.

Now as he watched a plane taxiing on the runway, he recognised the rounded wings, short nose, and twin propellers of an Avro Anson, the planes used to train fighter pilots during the war.

He was transfixed as the Anson sped up, hurtling down the runway until it reached that breath-taking moment when its wheels left the ground.

He was mesmerised by the soaring plane and the distinctive low buzz of its engines. He thought about the power needed to make a metal machine lift from the ground and sail through the air. How was it one moment fixed to the earth's surface and the next second rising upwards?

Although Cres was a fast learner, he didn't want to use that to show off. It was understanding how things worked that really motivated him.

Cres could watch planes all day, but he also wanted to go fishing.

He used a shovel to dig near the vegetable patch where there were lots of worms for bait. After filling his container with worms and dirt he grabbed his fishing rod and tackle from the shed.

Spotting his mother standing at the kitchen window, Cres tapped on the glass then held up his rod to show he was going fishing. She waved and smiled. Meg trusted him to be back before tea, hopefully with fish.

As Cres walked out the gate and down the road towards the town and the river, Prince bounded beside him. They went to Cres's favourite fishing spot near where the Evans River met the sea. Cres knew fish hid in the deep holes in this part of the river.

Cres loaded his hook with worms until it was completely covered by their writhing bodies. He'd once asked his dad if it hurt the worms. 'How would you feel if I put a hook through you?' the matter-of-fact Albert had replied.

Cres cast out his line then sat on a log with Prince beside him in the dappled shade, listening to waves on the nearby beach and waiting for the tell-tale pull on the line.

A twitch of the rod caught Cres's attention. He wasn't sure if he'd imagined the movement, but then the rod bent. He reeled in his line and flipped a good-sized silvery bream onto the bank. He killed the fish so it wouldn't suffer longer than necessary, before placing it in his bucket. Then he prepared his line to try his luck again.

After catching two more fish, Cres decided to head home, this time along the beach. The white sand was edged by dunes covered in sparse grass, behind which dark green scrub grew. The view of sand, scrub and sea curved ahead for kilometres in front of him.

On the water, white prawn trawlers were coming back to the jetty. Locals would meet the boats and buy fresh prawns from the fishermen.

Cres was tired and his gear felt heavy. It was a sunny day, and the sand was hot. Cres's feet slid in his sandals, and his shirt stuck to his skin. To his right the blue ocean looked cool and inviting. The temptation was too great. Dumping his gear on the sand, he took off his shirt and sandals and ran straight into the sea, enjoying the shock of cold water against his bare skin.

After swimming out past the small breaking waves, he rolled onto his back and stared up at the blue sky. A small twin-engine plane flew overhead. Cres imagined the pilot looking down at the ocean and perhaps making out a small kid floating below.

I'll be up there one day, he thought. I'll be a pilot. He was sure of it.

When he got out, Prince was waiting patiently. Cres hadn't brought a towel, but it didn't matter on such a warm day. The breeze would dry his clothes before he reached home.

As he walked, his wet clothes chaffed a little against his skin, but at least he felt cooler. Still full of energy, Prince bounded along near the water, seeming surprised every time the waves chased him up the shore. He brought a piece of driftwood to Cres, who took it from the dog's mouth and threw it underarm up the beach. Prince set off running after it.

A man was walking along the beach towards them, a towel slung over his shoulder. Prince noticed the man too, dropped his stick and ran towards him. Cres called out, 'Prince, come!' but the dog either didn't hear because of the wind, or was too excited to obey.

Cres ran as fast as he could with his fishing equipment, but Prince had already jumped on the stranger with his wet, sandy paws.

Cres caught up and said sharply, 'Down Prince!' and finally, Prince obeyed. 'Sorry,' he said to the man, who luckily didn't seem annoyed.

'Not to worry. Good catch?'

'Bream,' Cres said, showing him the fish.

Cres recognised the man as the doctor who lived in the large house in Woodburn. Once Cres had stepped on a broken bottle on the jetty and the doctor had lanced his foot to remove the glass.

The doctor obviously didn't recognise him, but Cres wasn't surprised. A country GP was an important man in the community and Cres was just a kid. On the beach without his formal suit and intimidating equipment, the doctor seemed more like an ordinary person.

'What's your name, son?' asked the doctor.

'Creswell.'

'No, I mean your first name.'

Cres fought down annoyance. He knew his name was unusual. The priest had refused to baptise him Creswell, so his parents switched his middle and first names. According to the Catholic Church, he was 'John Creswell' but that wasn't his real name.

'Creswell is my first name.'

'Is it a family name?'

'No, I'm named after my dad's commanding officer in the war—Randolph Creswell.'

'Have you met your namesake?'

Cres shook his head. Randolph Creswell died in Palestine in 1917. He was 27.

The doctor seemed to understand.

'We lost too many good men.'

Cres nodded. Every family had a relative who died or was wounded in one of the wars. At school they were always being told about the sacrifices young men had made for their freedom. And how lucky they were to live in peacetime Australia.

'Anyway, I'd better get home,' said Cres.

'Good lad.'

Arriving home, Cres took the fish straight to the outside laundry. His mother wouldn't want them inside until they were cleaned and filleted.

Cres was always happy when he brought home fish for the family. His grandma said eating fish was good for the brain. Cres had asked her why, but frustratingly, she didn't have a reason. As he gutted, scaled, and filleted the catch, Cres looked at the flesh, and wondered how it could help brains. Hopefully, he'd learn things like that at high school.

In the 19th century, scientists thought eating fish was good for the brain because brain matter is high in phosphorus and so is fish. This link was later disproved, but many people continued to believe it into the 20th century. Later, Cres would find out there is a different reason why seawater fish are good for people's brains.

Removing his sandals at the door and brushing the sand off his feet, Cres headed into the house. His mother was pressing his school uniform on the ironing board, which was covered by a brown army blanket.

His father had used the blanket in the deserts of the Middle East during the war, where the searingly hot daytime temperatures plunged to freezing at night.

Cres held out the fish for his mother to see. They were perfect fillets of white flesh, tinged with pink in the middle.

She nodded and said, 'Very good. Thanks. In the kitchen please and wash your hands.'

Sitting in an armchair, Albert was reading the paper. He laughed and Meg said, 'What's funny?'

'They're giving kids camel rides on the beach.' He held up the paper to show them.

Cres came over to see the black and white photo of three children sitting on a camel. The children leaned forward, their faces grinning.

'And they're charging sixpence!' said Albert. 'Waste of money getting on one of those stinking, bad-tempered brutes.'

Cres knew that since the war, his father hated camels. Albert had joined the Light Horse Regiment, but had later been recruited to the Camel Corp. Although the camels were useful in the desert, they didn't win hearts like horses did.

That evening, Albert was in the rare mood to talk about war so Cres sat and listened as his dad told stories of meeting **Lawrence of Arabia** and seeing the pyramids in Egypt. Margaret came to listen too because she was always interested in history.

Albert described seeing human bones in the trenches from wars fought thirty years previously. He spoke about awful things like terrible wounds and thirst that was so bad, men's tongues swelled.

> Thomas Edward Lawrence was a British intelligence officer who became known as **Lawrence of Arabia**. He fought with Arab guerrilla forces during World War I against the Turkish forces. Before the war he had been an archaeologist and photographer.

'Why did you go?' asked Margaret.

'It was your duty. You couldn't be cold-footed.'

Cres knew his father would never be a coward.

Albert had even tried to sign up for World War II but was rejected for health reasons.

'But how did you put up with it?' asked Margaret.

'When it got bad, I'd imagine coming back to my family in Maryborough. That got me through.'

'What was it like when you did come home?' asked Margaret.

'There was a band and a reception for me at the town hall!' said Albert. 'Very fancy.'

Their mother came into the room and announced, 'I spoke to Jean today. Father O'Connor will be saying Mass tomorrow.'

She looked at the family, expecting a reaction.

Margaret and Cres exchanged looks. Father O'Connor was the son of their mother's friend. His entry to the priesthood was a source of great pride.

'You know Father O'Connor studied in Rome?' said Meg.

'Yes, you've told us,' said Margaret.

'He met the Pope!' their mother exclaimed proudly, walking back towards the kitchen.

Cres said quietly, 'So he thinks he's God.'

Margaret and Albert laughed.

Meg turned back around. 'You're lucky I didn't hear that! Anyway, come on through, tea's ready.'

The meal was delicious, and Cres was proud that he'd provided food for everyone.

It had been a perfect day. In hard times in the future, Cres would remember days like this, and hope for better days again. It would get him through.

3

Operation

The next year life changed for Cres when his family moved from Evans Head to the nearby town of Lismore. Cres started school at the Marist College, which was a bigger school where he could play sport like cricket and football. He also studied science, including chemistry and physics, which he loved.

One cool spring morning Cres rode his bike away from the newsagent, his satchel full of newspapers to deliver.

He usually enjoyed riding the empty streets of Lismore before other people woke up. With no traffic, he could hear the birds chortling in the trees. But on this day, their chirping was making his headache worse. His stomach hurt too, and he felt dizzy.

He might be hungry. After all, he hadn't eaten anything for breakfast.

He stopped and took a banana out of his bag. He chewed the claggy fruit then forced himself to swallow, nearly gagging.

If anything, the banana had made him feel sicker, but Cres got back on his bike. His legs ached and his satchel felt really heavy. It took all his determination to finish his paper round.

After delivering the final paper he couldn't hold on any longer. He stood over a garden bed throwing up the banana, hoping the homeowner was asleep and not looking out their window. He could lose his job for this.

When he arrived back home his mother was surprised to see him. 'Cres, shouldn't you be at school?'

'I feel sick,' he said. 'I need to lie down. I'll go to school soon.'

Meg followed him to his bedroom and pulled back the bedcovers. Cres sat on a chair to take off his shoes but it hurt to bend. He lay on the bed still dressed in his school uniform, and his mother covered him with the sheet and blanket.

'Are you going to be sick?'

'I think so.'

When Meg returned to his bedroom with a bucket, Cres sat up and vomited again, then lay down and shut his eyes. He'd rest for a moment, then get up.

Cres slept briefly but woke feeling terrible. There was nothing left to vomit, but he retched into the bucket.

His mother came back looking worried. 'We should take you to the doctor.'

Cres didn't want to go to the family GP in Lismore. The doctor, who was known as Reddo Ryan, was a loud man, full of stories about how everything was worse during the war.

'But, I'm better,' Cres said weakly.

Meg wasn't fooled. She pulled off the covers and told him to get up.

At the surgery Dr Ryan prodded his stomach, which hurt and made Cres wince. He also asked lots of questions.

Then, the doctor delivered his verdict, 'Appendicitis. I'll have to operate.'

'When?' asked Meg.

'As soon as possible. We can't risk the **appendix** bursting.'

> The **appendix** is a finger-shaped pouch near where the small and large intestines meet. The appendix doesn't perform a vital function and humans can live long, healthy lives without one. Appendicitis is an inflammation of the appendix. Surgery to remove the appendix is a common treatment.

Meg frowned.

'Don't worry, Mrs Eastman,' said Dr Ryan, 'it's very safe at the hospital. You should've seen the conditions I operated under during the war! I took out my first appendix in an army tent!'

Meg looked reassured. Cres wanted it to be over.

For the next few hours Cres followed everyone's instructions while miserable and in pain. He couldn't think about anything but wanting to feel better.

Finally, he lay on the operating table.

'I'll put a mask over your face now,' explained Dr Ryan. 'It contains the anaesthetic chemical.'

'What's the chemical?' asked Cres.

'It's called diethyl ether,' said Dr Ryan. 'You're lucky! During the war I once took off a fellow's leg with no anaesthetic at all! He bit into a stick while we got on with it. Took five men to hold him down!'

A nurse squeezed Cres's hand. 'You'll feel better soon,' she promised.

When Dr Ryan placed a mask over his face, he could smell the chemical. It had a pungent but sweet aroma and felt suffocating.

'Stay calm, take deep breaths,' encouraged the nurse. 'You're doing really well.'

But the anaesthetic wasn't working. Cres wasn't falling asleep. He slowed down his breathing, trying to stay calm. He thought about lying on his back in the ocean, staring at the endless blue sky.

When he woke up, the sickly-sweet gas smell was still in his nostrils and his stomach still hurt. A wave of nausea engulfed him.

'I'm going to be sick!'

A nurse quickly put a basin under his chin, but the bitter liquid dribbled down his face and onto his neck as he coughed and spluttered.

He lay back on the pillow. The nurse dabbed him with a damp cloth.

Later in the day, his mother came to visit. Cres was relieved to see her.

'How are you?' she asked.

Cres grimaced, 'All right'.

'Dr Ryan said the operation went well.'

It didn't feel as if it went well to Cres.

He suddenly remembered his paper round. He'd be in trouble if he didn't show up. 'Someone needs to tell Mr Kennedy at the newsagents I can't come tomorrow.'

'Don't worry,' said Meg. 'I've already spoken to him. That nice boy, Patrick Kirk, will take over for you.'

'For the rest of the week?'

'No, permanently.'

'Oh, no!'

Meg looked confused. 'But you couldn't keep doing it, anyway. You'll be changing schools next year.'

Cres turned his head to the side, facing the bright white wall. Everything was changing. He couldn't stay a kid forever, but he thought he had a little longer.

Another wave of nausea passed through him. 'I'm going to be sick!' he croaked. Meg handed him the basin just in time.

4

Expectations

After Cres's first day back at school following his operation, he walked to his grandparent's house. His grandmother was pruning roses near the front gate when he arrived. Cres remembered how Prince would wait for him at the gate after school. Prince had died of a snake bite before they left Evans Head and Cres missed him terribly.

'How was school?' asked Grandma, taking off her gardening gloves.

'It was fine.'

'And how's your tummy feeling?' she asked.

'Better, thanks,' he said.

Grandma smiled and said, 'Very good. We were so worried about you, Cressy. Come inside.'

Cres flinched at being called Cressy. He hated it, but he wouldn't say anything.

Grandma went to the kitchen while Cres sat at the table. Hung on the wall opposite was a picture of Jesus Christ, in a dark oval frame. Jesus had sad eyes and his head was tilted to one side. In the centre of Jesus's chest was his heart, surrounded by thorns and dripping blood.

On the mantlepiece were framed family photos and, as usual, Cres's eye was drawn to one particular photo: a black-and-white portrait of a young boy with fair hair. His brother, Alistair.

Eight-year-old Alistair had become sick and died only a few months after the photo was taken. The cause of Alistair's illness wasn't known, but it was likely an infection after a knee injury. Once antibiotics became widely available this could be treated, but in 1940 it took the life of a beautiful young boy.

Grandma came back. 'Such a handsome, golden-haired boy,' she said sadly, looking at the photo.

Cres smiled at the familiar words.

'You know he was staying with us when he died?' said Grandma. 'You were a tiny baby. The older children came to stay with us to give your mother a rest.'

Cres nodded, he'd heard this story before. Barbara remembered going to the shop to buy cold lemonade and ice for Alistair. But it hadn't helped. Alistair had got sicker and was taken to hospital.

'Poor Muggie,' said Grandma, using her pet name for his mother. 'A mother never gets over losing her child.'

Cres knew this was true. Cres's parents loved their three living children but the sadness for their first-born never went away.

Alistair was good at sports and popular, everyone said that. He would be 18 by now. Cres stared at the photo of the boy, trying to imagine him grown up. Even though he couldn't remember his brother, the sadness of Alistair's early death was part of his life.

Grandma put a piece of cake in front of him.

'Eat up, Cressy,' said Grandma.

After thinking about Alistair, Cres didn't feel hungry, but he took a bite of the cake anyway.

'Do you know what school you'll be going to next year?' asked Grandma.

Cres shook his head. He swallowed then said, 'I have my exams next week. I'll know more when I get my results.'

'Well, you study hard,' urged Grandma. 'A scholarship would really help your parents.'

Cres nodded. He knew and hoped he wouldn't let them down.

*

Cres was waiting with the other boys outside the classroom. It was the final week at school for the year and they'd already finished their exams. They were running down the clock until the holidays.

'Hey, Cres!' said Fergus, a red-headed kid Cres played cricket with. 'Show us your scar!'

Cres shook his head. He wanted to forget everything about his operation. Occasionally, he'd smell something that reminded him of the anaesthetic and feel ill again.

'Come on!' said Harry. 'Show us!'

Reluctantly, Cres lifted his shirt to reveal the jagged red scar on his right side.

'Wow!' Fergus said, with a shudder. 'Looks like you were sawn in half!'

'Did it hurt?' asked Harry.

Cres shrugged. Of course, it had hurt.

'Brother!' yelled the boy on lookout and the kids quickly formed a neat line.

Brother Fabian approached the class and walked up to Cres. He laid a hand on his shoulder and said, 'The headmaster would like to see you.'

As Cres walked to the headmaster's office, he felt nervous, wondering what he'd done wrong.

The door was open when he arrived. Sitting at his big wooden desk the headmaster waved him in. To Cres's surprise his mother was in the office, sitting in a straight-backed wooden chair.

His stomach dropped to his shoes. Oh, no, this must be serious.

'Have a seat, Creswell,' said the headmaster.

Cres sat down on a wooden chair beside Meg. Although it was a warm day, she was wearing her best dress, with long sleeves. Her face was shiny with sweat.

Smiling, the headmaster declared, 'Creswell, I have good news. As your teachers expected, you've done extremely well in your final examinations.'

'Thank you,' said Cres.

'You've won two scholarships. One from the New South Wales State Government and one from the Catholic Board of Education.'

Meg was sitting very straight in her chair. Although she didn't turn to look at him, Cres could tell she was pleased and that made him feel warm inside. She'd been through a lot, losing her first-born son, and caring for his dad who was often ill, so Cres was glad he could make her proud.

The headmaster continued, 'In this light, we recommend you attend La Valla Juniorate, a Marist college in Bowral.'

'Bowral?' said Cres. He'd never been there; he only knew it was the country town where Don Bradman grew up. Bradman famously honed his batting skills hitting a golf ball against a tank stand with a cricket stump.

'Can I catch the bus?'

The headmaster laughed and Meg smiled. 'It's two hours south of Sydney,' Meg explained. 'You'd live at the school. It's a boarding school.'

'It's a wonderful place,' said the headmaster. 'It offers a good education and fosters the spiritual growth of students. Do you know what a Juniorate is?'

Cres shook his head.

'It's a school that prepares boys for a spiritual life of service and to take vows of poverty, obedience and chastity.'

Cres knew what the first two were, but he wasn't sure about chastity. It had something to do with priests not getting married. That seemed fine to him. He was only 12 and never thought about getting married anyway.

'After completing their school studies at the Juniorate boys are well-prepared to move to the Novitiate to become Marist brothers,' continued the headmaster.

Cres didn't know what to say. His mouth was dry. He tried to catch Meg's eye, but she was still looking at the headmaster.

Cres noticed a glass of iced water on the desk. The outside of the glass was covered in beads of liquid. He wished he could grab it and take a long drink.

'The boys have a wonderful life,' said the headmaster. 'You could join the football and cricket teams and learn hockey. The Mittagong campus is surrounded by bushland and students swim in the dam in the warmer months.'

'What about school?' asked Cres. He wanted to study more science. He wanted to understand how planes stayed in the air and why humans needed oxygen.

'La Valla Juniorate teaches the same subjects as any other school. I know you have a talent for maths and science. The teachers will help you develop this.'

'It sounds good,' says Cres hesitatingly. 'But what about closer schools?'

The headmaster didn't answer immediately. The clock on the mantlepiece ticked loudly. Cres lifted one of his legs and felt the skin on the back of his knees sticking to the wooden chair.

Meg gave him a look that said, 'stop fidgeting'.

The headmaster coughed and said, 'I have a finely tuned ability to spot a religious vocation in young boys. Creswell, you have the character required for religious life. From my personal experience, it is a very rewarding one.'

'I want to be a pilot—'

Cres's mother interrupted, 'This is an honour, Cres. A vocation is a gift from God. It's wonderful to be called to serve.'

The headmaster nodded. 'Yes, and you'll receive a much finer education than your parents could afford otherwise. Then you can give back to the community by teaching.'

It was a lot to take in. Cres put his hand on his stomach. Through his shirt he felt the jagged ridge of his scar. He'd already survived something difficult and that gave him confidence for the future.

'All right,' he agreed.

The headmaster smiled warmly at him, and his mother seemed pleased too. This must be the right decision. He'd play sport every day and live with boys his age. In books, kids at boarding school had midnight feasts and adventures.

Cres smiled at Meg and she smiled back.

'We'll miss you so much,' she said. 'But this is for the best.'

5

Goodbye

Cres stood on the footpath with his mother in front of the building that would be his school and home. La Valla Juniorate was a large two-storey mansion painted light pink with elaborate iron lace decorating the verandahs.

They walked up the driveway to the front door where Meg pressed the brass bell. Through the glass panes, a blurry figure became visible, then an elderly, white-haired man opened the door. He was dressed like Cres's teachers in Lismore, in a long black robe, called a soutane, with a white square at his neck. He had a cord around his waist and a large cross hung from his neck.

'Good morning. I'm Meg Eastman and this is Creswell Eastman.'

'Pleased to meet you. I'm Brother William, Master of Juniors.'

Cres peered past the man into the grand entranceway where he could see elaborate plaster-work on the ceiling and in the centre, a sparkling chandelier.

As they entered, the brother pointed to a statue of Mary on the hallstand with the words engraved below: *Ad Jesum per Mariam.*

'Do you know what this means?' he asked.

'To Jesus through Mary,' answered Cres. It was the Marist motto, which he'd seen at his school in Lismore.

Brother William nodded curtly. 'Quite right. Now, I will take you through to the dormitories.'

He stepped outside onto the portico. They followed him along the side of the house to a weatherboard section of the building.

'This is the new extension,' Brother William explained. 'There's a chapel underneath and above are the boys' dormitories.'

Brother William led them up the stairs to the first-floor landing, where he opened a door.

Cres stepped into a long room with a row of black iron beds against the wall. Each bed had a dark wooden cupboard beside it. A statue of Mary was set into a recess in the wall opposite. The room smelled of fresh paint.

Pointing to the fourth bed from the door, the brother announced, 'That will be yours, Creswell. And that's your locker to store personal items.'

'It looks very comfortable,' said Meg. 'Have the other boys arrived?'

'Yes,' said Brother William, 'they're out on a picnic.'

'How lovely!' said Meg.

'We give the boys a balance of study, work and recreation. It helps them avoid the storms and temptations of adolescence.'

They returned to the main house for tea and biscuits. Brother William told Meg about the students from the Solomon Islands who attended La Valla Juniorate.

'Australia must be very different,' said Meg. 'Are they homesick?'

'We keep our boys busy,' he said. 'It keeps sentimental thoughts away.'

Cres only half listened. He kept thinking that soon his mother would leave. He'd be alone.

When the time came, they hugged tightly.

'You be good,' Meg said, her voice muffled in his shoulder. She sounded as if she might cry.

'Of course,' he replied, trying to sound cheerful, but tears threatened to come.

'I'll see you at Christmas,' she said.

That was almost too much. Christmas was eleven months away. Cres knew if he spoke, he would cry, so he nodded instead.

As he watched Meg walk away down the school's driveway, heading to the train station, her figure became blurry as his eyes filled with tears.

Brother William turned to him and said, 'You may go to your dormitory and unpack.'

The dorm was eerily still and quiet. The statue of Mary opposite Cres's bed stared at him with her piercing blue gaze. He unpacked his suitcase then sat on the bed and took out his going away present, a boys' adventure story in the popular Biggles series titled, *Biggles Fails to Return*.

He read the inscription on the first page again: *Don't you dare fail to return, Cres! Love Barbara and Margaret.*

Turning to the first chapter, he was soon absorbed in the adventures of James Bigglesworth, adventurer and pilot.

Some time later, he heard voices in the corridor before the door burst open. Boys streamed in and went to their cupboards with a flurry of banging doors and conversation.

Then they started to leave again. Someone said to him, 'Come on. Mass.'

Cres followed the boys downstairs to the chapel. At the entrance, he dipped his hand in the holy water and made the sign of the cross. Before sliding into a pew he genuflected towards the altar, bending one knee to the ground. At least he knew what to do in church.

The priest began his solemn procession to the altar.

Cres thought about his mother. She'd be in Sydney waiting for the overnight train to Lismore. He felt panicky being so far away from his family, but he fought the feeling down.

The **Mass** was said in Latin. The words and accompanying gestures were the same in every Catholic church, which Cres found comforting.

In Australia, the Catholic church service, called **Mass**, was said in Latin until 1967 when English began to be used.

During the sermon, which was in English, the priest announced, 'There are some new boys here today. Please welcome them and help them settle into their new life here. Let the blessed virgin Mary be your example as you care for them.'

The priest then spoke about chastity. The boys were told they risked hellfire if they had impure thoughts or committed wanton acts.

After Mass they went to the dining room for the evening meal of meat and vegetables. They sat at a long table with Brother William at the head and three other Marist brothers beside him. Everyone ate in silence.

Cres wasn't hungry, but he forced himself to eat—he had always been told that wasting food was a sin.

Cres remembered how at home during meals his sister Barbara told amusing stories about her day as a nurse. Or Margaret talked about her commercial studies at the Lismore Technical College. Sometimes his sisters teased him. He thought he hated it, but now he really missed it.

After eating, the boys cleared the tables then filed to their dormitory, led by a solemn Brother William. Cres hadn't seen him smile all day.

Walking into the dormitory Cres heard an explosive shout.

'What's this!'

Cres saw Brother William holding the Biggles book above his head.

'Is this yours, Creswell Eastman?'

'Yes, Brother.'

'Why was it lying on your bed?'

'I didn't realise—'

'You see this!' Brother William said, gesturing towards his locker. 'I told you to store personal items there.'

'Yes, Brother,' said Cres.

'I am confiscating this book until you can follow school rules. Tomorrow, you'll be on duty to clean the grease traps.'

The man turned and swept out. The other boys continued getting ready for bed, as if nothing unusual had happened, while Cres stood still, shocked by the brother's reaction to a small mistake.

When he looked at the statue of Mary, her blue eyes were blank.

'Come on then, I'll show you the bathrooms,' said a voice. 'I'm Kevin, by the way.'

Cres turned and saw a boy with a freckled face and friendly smile. 'I'm Creswell, or Cres,' he said.

He followed Kevin to the bathroom where they stood side by side at the sinks and brushed their teeth. Kevin smiled a frothy smile at Cres.

Walking back to the dormitory, Cres asked, 'What's a grease trap anyway?'

'It's where the grease collects from the pipes. It gets clogged up, so you have to scrape it out. The smell is the worst part.'

In bed, with the lights out, Cres thought about his family and home in Lismore. He longed for his comfortable room, with his shelf of books and model aeroplanes on display. He felt like crying but didn't want anyone to hear.

Cres was a fast learner. He already knew that at La Valla Juniorate everything needed to be kept locked away, including your feelings.

*

Over the next few months Cres got used to life at boarding school. Every day was long. Up at 5.30, jobs and prayers before breakfast. Then a full day of school studies. They played sport in the afternoons—cricket, football, and hockey—which was fun. This was followed by more jobs, lectures, dinner, homework, and bed. Repeat.

At least being busy kept Cres's mind off missing home too much.

One winter afternoon Cres bounded up the steps to his dormitory, a parcel under his arm.

He rubbed his hands together to warm them up. He'd spent the last hour chopping firewood and, although his body had warmed up with the effort, his hands were white and numb.

The parcel was addressed in Barbara's writing. He loved hearing from his sisters. Sitting on his bed, he ripped the parcel open.

'What's that?' asked Kevin.

'New Biggles,' said Cres, holding up *Biggles in the Special Air Police.*

'Can I read it after you?' asked Kevin.

'Of course.'

Cres quickly read the letter from Barbara. She told him about a film she'd seen, and how she'd been on a holiday with friends at the beach. She said Mum was well and Dad had his usual troubles. She ended with encouraging words:

I know school is hard, but we're so proud of you. Your half-year reports were fantastic. Keep it up, and Christmas will be here before you know it. See you soon. Love Barbara

Soon! It might seem soon to Barbara, but four months until the holidays seemed forever to Cres.

The door creaked and the boys looked up to see Brother William standing in the doorway.

'Creswell,' he said, 'please come with me.'

Cres had no idea why Brother William wanted to speak to him. Sometimes boys had private tutoring sessions, which he'd been warned to avoid. He didn't know how though. If a brother told you to go somewhere, you had to obey. Cres put the book and letters into his locker then followed the teacher.

In his office, Brother William told Cres that his father was very sick and that Cres needed to pack his bag and catch the train to Lismore the next day.

'Do you understand?' asked Brother William.

'Yes, Brother.'

'All right, you can go now.'

Cres stood up and walked towards the door.

'And Creswell,' said Brother William.

Cres turned, longing for a kind word.

'Close the door after you.'

*

The next day, Cres got off the train at Sydney's Central Station, bewildered by the noise and commotion. Last time he'd been there was with his mother, and she'd led the way. He felt lost on his own.

He breathed a lungful of smoke from the steam engine and coughed.

Cres needed to buy a ticket for the overnight train to Murwillumbah, wait five hours for the next train, then travel for 12 hours to Lismore.

People strode confidently along the platform, busy and important. Cres followed the crowd, his suitcase bumping against his legs. He came into the main concourse with its cavernous domed ceiling. Billboards hung from the curved iron railings advertising 'McWilliam's Wines' and 'Vincent's APC', which was a pain medication.

A big clock with Roman numerals hung from a wire and showed the time was three minutes past two.

Then Cres spotted a large sign reading 'Tickets' at the far end of the hall.

He joined a queue behind a lady wearing a fur coat. It reminded him of his mother's coat, the one his dad gave her as a wedding present.

Cres felt a lump in his throat. His dad. His dad was sick in hospital.

After buying his ticket, Cres checked his suitcase into a locker then wondered what to do next. His teacher had told him to wait in the train station, but it was too smoky and noisy. Anyway, he needed to do something to stop worrying.

Following the signs to the Elizabeth Street exit, he left the station's gloom and stepped out into the busy, bright street. He stopped to look around.

A man nearly bumped into him. 'Hey! Don't stand in the middle of the footpath!'

Cres started walking, without a clear plan. After a few blocks he came to a park where he sat on a bench to eat a sandwich the school had packed.

A large man with a bushy black beard came and sat beside him. He smiled, and Cres smiled back.

'Shouldn't you be in school?' asked the man.

'I'm going home to visit my dad,' explained Cres. 'He's sick.'

'I'm sorry to hear that. Where are you going?'

'Lismore. I'm catching a train tonight.'

'That's a long way for a little fella alone. Do you have the fare?'

'Yes, thanks. I've already bought my ticket. I have extra money for emergencies too.'

The man shuffled a little closer on the bench saying, 'You don't want to hang around the park all day. I know a little place near here. I could buy you a hot drink.'

The man smiled, but Cres felt uncomfortable. He didn't want to be rude, though, so he agreed.

He began walking with the man, but couldn't shake his bad feelings.

'Actually,' said Cres. 'I'd better get back to the station.'

The man grabbed Cres's arm and said, 'Don't be silly. It's not far.'

Cres shook off the man's grip and ran. The street was busy, but Cres darted between people. 'Sorry!' he cried as he bumped into a lady carrying a round hatbox.

He looked behind him and even though he couldn't see the man, he ran for two more blocks, just to be safe, his heart pounding.

Cres spent the rest of the afternoon wandering around Sydney. He bought hot chips and ate them while admiring the impressive steel structure of the **Sydney Harbour Bridge**.

The **Sydney Harbour Bridge** is one of the longest steel-arch bridges in the world. It is 500 metres long with four railway tracks, a highway and pedestrian and cycle paths. It was completed in 1932.

Finally, it was time to catch the train. After collecting his suitcase, Cres went to Platform 8 where the train waited, its black engine hissing and billowing smoke.

He walked to a third-class carriage and stepped in, making his way down the narrow corridor until he found an empty compartment where he sat down by the window. After spending the afternoon alone in the city, it was a relief to be somewhere safe and enclosed.

Cres wondered what would happen when he arrived in Lismore. He hoped he'd be told that his dad wasn't as ill as they'd feared. After all, Albert was tough. He'd survived the battle of the Nek at Gallipoli. He'd charged from the trench over the bodies of his friends, and been shot, but he'd survived. His father was lucky, tough, and brave.

The train sounded its whistle. Cres felt the carriage shudder underneath him as the train began to chug slowly out of the station and through Sydney's suburbs, increasing speed as it left the outskirts of the city. There were no lights outside now, and the countryside was black. Looking at the window, all he could see was his reflection.

When Cres arrived in Lismore the next day, he visited his dad in the hospital. Albert lay in the bed, his body smaller than usual, his skin grey. He was struggling to breathe. Cres was shocked to realise that his father didn't even know he had visitors.

As he sat beside the bed, Cres understood that Albert wouldn't be lucky this time. This illness would be his last.

'Dad's dying', he thought over and over again. But he couldn't fully comprehend that his life and family were changing forever.

He knew his dad was sick, even before he left for boarding school, but he hadn't been prepared to say goodbye forever, or for the sadness that would come for himself and his family.

After his dad's funeral Cres made the long journey back to boarding school alone.

6

Back

Cres looked towards the boundary where spectators were crowding, watching the game. Actually, at this moment they were all watching him.

The Under 16s Marist College team was playing Chevalier College and the scores were tied. There was no time left in the game, but Cres had a free kick. If he scored now his school would earn a place in the final. If he missed, his team would lose, and their 1955 football season would be over.

It felt like the most important moment in his life. Cres looked at the football, then up at the goal posts, which seemed very far away. Cres loved playing, but at moments like these the pressure almost felt too much.

His heart thumped, and his head felt fuzzy.

'You'll never make it!' called a man's gruff voice from the boundary line. Cres turned and saw an older man wearing a priest's collar and a woollen beanie in Chevalier College colours.

Cres tried to ignore him.

'If you kick that, I'll give you my best **rosary beads**,' the man yelled, holding up a set of red beads on a silver chain. The small baubles shone like jewels.

Rosary beads are used for counting a set of Catholic prayers called the rosary. Beads for counting prayers are also used by many other religions including Islam, Hinduism and Buddhism.

Alright then, thought Cres. He looked at the ball. He looked back up at the goalposts. He focused, he kicked, and the ball sailed through.

They'd won!

He ran to his teammates who slapped him on the back and hugged him. Then Cres went over to the priest who'd tried, and failed, to put him off.

'What do you want?' said the man.

'I kicked the goal, Father,' said Cres.

'So what?'

'The rosary beads?'

The priest handed them over, grumping, 'They're only my second best really.'

Cres grinned and ran back to his teammates.

*

Cres was getting ready for church on Sunday morning. He was home for the summer holidays which was the only time he got to see his family—just once a year. But it always seemed easy to slip into the old family routines again.

He opened his top drawer and pulled out his rosary beads.

'Are you ready?' called his mother.

Cres quickly tucked in his shirt and smoothed his hair.

'Yes! Coming!' he called, walking out of his room.

Spotting the beads, Meg said, 'What're they?'

Cres held them out for her to see. Meg reached for them and admired the red stones and silver cross.

'They're beautiful! Where did you get them?'

Cres hesitated, he didn't want to brag, but he couldn't explain having the rosary beads without mentioning his winning goal against Chevalier College.

He told the story and finished with, 'Anyway, the goal went through, and we won.' He shrugged, 'So, he gave me these.'

Meg looked surprised.

Cres felt himself blushing. He didn't usually tell stories about himself.

Finally, Meg responded, 'I didn't know you liked football.'

She handed the rosary beads back.

Cres was shocked. He loved football. How could his mother not know that?

He wished he'd kept the story to himself. When people didn't understand it made the moment feel smaller and less important.

Cres slipped the beads into his pocket, fingering the smooth, cold stones as he remembered that day. He knew his mother was proud of his achievements at school, and she was thrilled when he came home for the holidays. But she didn't follow every detail of his life like some mothers did.

It doesn't matter, Cres told himself. Kicking the winning goal was a moment of joy and triumph and the rosary beads were a reminder it had happened. He didn't need anyone else's praise to know what he'd done.

*

Back at school, Cres was playing in one of the first games of the season. He caught the ball and ran towards the goals. Hearing heavy footfalls on the sodden grass behind him, he picked up speed.

The feet got closer and closer. He heard the runner's gasping breath. Arms grabbed for him, knocking him sideways, but he still had the ball. He turned to keep running but the arms caught him around the waist. Cres's back slammed hard against the goal post. The ball rolled from his hands.

Cres slid to the ground. Shards of pain radiated from his lower back, up into his shoulders. He smelt the wet grass and earth.

His teammate, David, ran over to him, offering a hand up.

But Cres couldn't take it. 'I've hurt my back,' he said, sounding strangely calm.

Cres was carried off on a stretcher, wincing in pain with the jolting movements.

*

Months later, Cres walked gingerly up the steps to a doctor's office in Sydney, accompanied by a teacher. His back injury still hadn't healed. He'd missed the rest of the football season and now cricket was starting, but he couldn't play. Sometimes, he struggled just to walk and move around.

His teacher spoke to the receptionist then they sat in the waiting room. Cres took out his chemistry homework and put his exercise book on his lap to write with his fountain pen. His back hurt, but he ignored it. Once he became interested in his work, the pain faded.

Cres wrote out equations for a chemistry practical lesson later in the week. They would use a method called titration to measure the concentration of vitamin C in orange juice. This involved slowly adding an iodine compound to a mixture of juice and starch. The iodine would react with the vitamin C. When there was no vitamin C left, a different reaction between iodine and starch happened which turned the mixture a blue-black colour.

If you carefully measured the quantity of iodine added before the solution went black, you could work out the concentration of vitamin C in the juice. The more iodine was needed, the higher the concentration of vitamin C.

Cres was excited to try the experiment later in the week. He loved being in the chemistry lab using the Bunsen burners, glass-stoppered solutions and powders. It was interesting to observe the reactions when chemicals were added together, and fascinating to understand why these happened.

'Creswell Eastman,' said a voice.

The doctor stood in the waiting room. He had dark, slicked back hair, a friendly smile and wore a white coat over a dark grey suit.

'That's me,' said Cres.

'I'm Dr Dwyer. Pleased to meet you, Creswell.'

Dr Dwyer peered at Cres's notebook. 'Ah! Chemistry. I remember my days of titrations. If I remember rightly that vitamin C titration can be a little unreliable.'

'Would you like me to come in, Doctor?' Cres's teacher asked.

'That's alright, Brother,' said Dr Dwyer. 'I'll examine Creswell first and speak to you later.'

Cres quickly put his book and pen away before following the specialist into the examination room.

Gesturing towards a seat, Dr Dwyer said, 'I've been told you have a back injury.'

Cres explained that his back had never fully recovered after being slammed into the goalpost months earlier.

Dr Dwyer pointed at the large envelope Cres held. 'Are they X-rays for me?'

Cres handed him the envelope. He had already examined the images himself, holding them up to the light at a window. They were studying human anatomy at school and he knew some names of the bones but had no idea what the X-ray said about his injury.

Dr Dwyer attached the X-ray to a light box on the wall and peered at it closely. Immediately, he seemed to understand what he was seeing. He murmured to himself and made notes.

'I'll examine you now,' he said. 'Please remove your shirt and sit here.'

Dr Dwyer felt Cres's spine. His fingers were cold as he probed, and made Cres flinch.

'Alright, you can put your shirt on.'

As Cres got dressed, Dr Dwyer said, 'So, what are you enjoying most at school?'

'Well, I liked sport. Until I had this injury. And science, particularly chemistry.'

'What would you like to do when you leave school?'

Cres was surprised by the question. No one ever asked him. Everything was assumed. 'I'm at the Marist Juniorate in Mittagong,' Cres explained.

Dr Dwyer sat down at his desk.

'I know that, but do you have a religious vocation?'

Cres wasn't sure. His mother, his teachers and his friends expected him to continue with religious training when he finished school. They expected him to move into the Novitiate to begin formal studies to become a Marist brother.

'Everyone thinks—' said Cres.

'But what do *you* want to do?'

Cres didn't know what to say. He'd love to be like Dr Dwyer, understanding how to read X-rays and helping patients.

'You don't have to decide now,' said Dr Dwyer. 'But keep thinking about it.'

After that visit, Cres wore a back brace for a few months and slowly, his injury improved. He visited Dr Dwyer for follow-up appointments, and each time he was impressed by the doctor's knowledge and desire to help people. The specialist was Catholic too, but he dedicated himself to helping people through medicine. It was a different kind of vocation.

Dr Dwyer always asked Cres how his studies were going and what he might do after school.

With every visit, Cres became more certain of his answer. He wanted to study science at university.

It was more than that though. He wanted to meet new people. He wanted to have a job, his own place to live, and maybe a family one day.

The problem was, it wasn't what his school or family expected. His mother was proud that her son was on track to become a Marist brother, and for her, there was nothing nobler than becoming a priest or brother.

But living with the brothers had shown Cres that the religious men weren't better than other people. It was the hypocrisy he couldn't stand: saying one thing and doing another. There was no way he wanted to become one of them.

If his dad was alive, it would have been different. Albert had seen the world and survived battles in war; he would have understood his son wanting more from life. They could have talked about what Cres wanted. Instead, Cres had to work it out by himself.

At the end of the year, when he returned home he broke the news to his family. He wouldn't become a Marist Brother. Instead, he'd apply to study science at Sydney University.

They were shocked. Cres's mother had always supported his education but no one in his family had been to university, and she didn't fully understand why he wanted to do this rather than have the glory of a religious life. But Cres had to make his own decisions. He didn't need other people's approval, even when he wanted it.

When Cres got his final year results, he discovered he'd won a scholarship to study for a Bachelor of Science at Sydney University. His sisters and mother were very pleased for him, and he was positive he'd made the right decision.

He was free and full of potential.

7

University

Cres crept out of his bedroom, a floorboard under the hall rug creaking. He opened the door to the kitchen.

Mr Johnson was already seated at the table eating eggs and bacon. Mrs Johnson was sitting, breastfeeding her youngest child. Embarrassed, Cres looked away.

He paid the Johnsons weekly rent for a shared bedroom in their house. In theory, this money also covered breakfast and dinner.

'Good morning,' said Cres.

Neither adult looked up, but Mr Johnson grunted.

Cres had hoped to be up before the couple, that way he could get his breakfast alone. With them in the kitchen he wasn't comfortable getting food, but he also couldn't ask Mrs Johnson to make him breakfast while she was feeding the baby.

So Cres said, 'I'm off to university now.'

'All right for some,' Mr Johnson replied.

On the way to the bus stop Cres thought about the Johnsons. He felt sorry for them, because they seemed unhappy, but living with them also made him unhappy. He felt unwelcome in the common areas, so he stayed in his small bedroom and studied sitting on his bed with books on his lap. This uncomfortable position had made his back injury flare up again.

Cres rarely ate with the Johnsons, but didn't have enough money to buy more than one meal a day, so he was often hungry. And after living and studying in Sydney for three years he still felt as if he didn't have a home. At least the Johnson's house was better than the boarding house he'd lived in previously. He was safe at the Johnson's.

At the bus stop Cres looked down the road and saw the green-and-yellow double-decker bus that went past the university towering above the cars.

Getting on the bus, Cres went to the top where it was quieter and the fumes from the exhaust less noticeable.

He got out his chemistry textbook and started to read—exams were coming up, so he used every spare moment to study.

At the stop closest to Sydney University, Cres got off the bus and walked past shops selling fruit and vegetables, a tobacconist and barber, then past a popular student café, the smell of coffee and bacon making his stomach rumble hungrily. Three young people sat at an outside table laughing and eating sandwiches. He didn't know if he was more jealous of their food, or their friendship.

The other Sydney Uni students seemed to fit in naturally. They seemed to know each other, possibly because they went to school together.

Cres had learned to be independent at boarding school but was still surrounded by friends and fellow boarders. At university, though, he sometimes felt truly alone. No one understood his situation. Most students were living in their family home or in the university colleges and most were from well-off families.

On the other hand, the people he boarded with, like the Johnsons, had difficult physical jobs and hard lives, and thought university students were snobs and slackers.

Cres had made it through the hard years of Catholic boarding school and escaped from the strict life of the Marist brothers. University was an exciting adventure, but it was also hard.

His sister, Barbara, suggested he join a cricket or football team, but he couldn't always afford the equipment or the travel to games.

Cres did play squash with Dr Dwyer, who had suggested it might help Cres's back injury. Dr Dwyer had given Cres a racquet and invited him to play at the University Club in Macquarie Street. The Club's members were wealthy, well-dressed professionals so Cres sometimes felt out of place, but he enjoyed playing with Dr Dwyer and discussing what he was studying.

On campus, Cres made his way to his chemistry lecture. He passed the Medical Faculty and was awed by the huge sandstone building and the manicured lawns surrounding it.

A group of students walked into the faculty, talking animatedly. Cres hoped that would be him next year. He had decided that he wanted to become a doctor. He imagined himself as a country GP, delivering babies, performing emergency surgery, and removing glass from children's feet. He felt he could really help people.

He didn't have enough money to continue his studies beyond his science degree, so Cres had applied for a full scholarship to study medicine from the Soldier's Children's Education Board. There had been lots of of interviews and tests. His first results on the IQ test were so high the examiners decided they were 'suspicious' and Cres had been asked to sit the test again. Now he was waiting to hear if he'd got the scholarship.

Cres continued to the Chemistry Building, which was one of the university's newer buildings—a modern seven-storey rectangular structure of glass and concrete.

Standing near the doorway of Lecture Theatre 2, Creswell looked up at the tiered seating, scanning for an empty spot. The room was already packed with students. He hoped he wouldn't have to stand at the back again.

He heard a voice call, 'Cres!'

Cres spotted his friend, who he'd met back in first year chemistry, waving to him from a seat near the back. Cres carefully made his way up the stairs and slid onto the wooden bench just as the lecturer came to the front and the room quietened.

The lecturer talked and wrote on the blackboard while the class took notes. There was no time to ask questions, and no tutorials. Luckily, Cres found the material fascinating and was able to keep up. He'd known many students who couldn't cope with the fast pace of learning and had dropped out.

When Cres arrived back at the Johnson's house later that day, he could hear the baby crying and an older child shouting. Going straight to his room and closing the door, he could still clearly hear the household in its usual evening chaos.

On Cres's bed was an envelope. He picked it up, realising it was from the government's Department of Repatriation. It was the results of his scholarship application. He quickly opened the envelope, shutting his eyes for a few seconds as he took out the letter and unfolded it. Then he opened his eyes and read:

Dear Mr Eastman,
We are pleased to inform you that you have been granted a full scholarship to study Medicine at the University of Sydney...

Cres sat on the bed, shock and relief washing over him. Then he read the rest of the letter. The scholarship would fund not just his fees but also books and a reasonable living allowance. He wouldn't have to bother his mother for extra money, or work gruelling part-time and holiday jobs to cover his costs. Next year was going to be different.

*

Cres wasn't sure he'd heard correctly.

'Pardon?' he said. 'You want me to do what?'

The Director of Anaesthetics repeated, 'Give the boy over there an ether anaesthetic.'

It was exactly what Cres had heard the first time. Ether was diethyl ether, the horrible chemical he remembered from having his appendix out.

'But, why?' Cres asked.

'Because he's having his tonsils out,' replied the director, sounding impatient. 'But why an ether anaesthetic?'

'Because, I need to say that I've seen you give one. It's part of your assessment. You do know how?'

'Of course,' Cres said quickly.

He'd won his scholarship to study medicine five years earlier and was now completing his anaesthetics training through St Vincent's Clinical School, which was part of the University of Sydney. He understood the principles of an ether anaesthetic. That wasn't the point.

'Wouldn't an intravenous anaesthetic be better for the kid?' asked Cres.

'I'm asking you to give an ether anaesthetic.'

Cres looked at his shoes. They were polished and shining because they had to be. Tutors threw medical students out for offences like scuffed shoes.

Cres remembered his appendix operation. The ether anaesthetic caused awful sickness, and he still shuddered at the smell. He wasn't going to do that to another person unless there was a good reason. He certainly wouldn't do it so someone could tick a box on a form.

Cres said, 'I'm not gonna do it.' His voice sounded firm, but he was sweating under his white coat.

'Very well.'

The Director of Anaesthetics swept off, his shoes squeaking on the linoleum.

That evening Cres felt heavy as he walked up the steps of Glen Mervyn House, a two-storey brown-brick boarding house in Randwick that was run by **Legacy**.

Legacy is a charity founded after World War I. It provides support to the children and partners of Australian Defence Force members killed or injured during service.

Glen Mervyn House was a good place to live. It was neat and orderly with some meals provided, and downstairs there was a quiet study area, separate from the recreation room. Compared to the other places Cres had lived in since coming to Sydney, it was five-star accommodation.

And he had a lot in common with the other boarders at Glen Mervyn House. They were country kids studying in the city, and they'd all lost a parent due to war. It was easy to make friends. In fact, moving into Glen Mervyn House changed Cres's life, and it finally felt as if he had a home in Sydney. He would never forget the support of Legacy.

Having enough money and a stable home also meant Cres had more freedom to play sport again, which was a good release and distraction from the pressures of study. He played cricket competitively and hockey socially, but football was still too risky for his back.

That day Cres wasn't in the mood to talk to the other residents, so he went straight to his bedroom. He lay on the neat, blue bedspread and stared at the high ceiling, running over the day's events in his head.

A few minutes later, the door opened and Cres's roommate came in.

'Hey, Cres, Annette's downstairs to see you.'

Cres sat up, feeling more cheerful. With everything that had happened that day he'd forgotten he'd arranged for his girlfriend to visit.

Cres and Annette sat in the wicker chairs on the porch, looking through the verandah's arches at the garden. He breathed in the smell of newly cut grass, reminding him of school sports ovals before a competition.

Cres was quiet. His confrontation with the Director of Anaesthetics playing on his mind.

'What's wrong?' asked Annette.

'Nothing.'

'Come on, it's not nothing.'

Cres wasn't used to having someone to talk to—he was used to dealing with problems on his own. He took a sip of tea.

'I think I'm in trouble.'

Annette listened without interrupting as he explained what had happened. He finished by saying, 'I'll probably have to report to the Medical Superintendent.'

Cres waited for Annette's response, expecting her to say he'd made a huge mistake.

'You did the right thing.'

'But what if I get kicked out of medicine?'

'You're the top student in your year. At worst, you'll get a telling off.'

He was still worried but felt lighter after talking about it. He felt good that Annette supported him standing up for what he believed was right, even if it put his own future at risk.

Cres had worked hard to get this far in his medical studies and he didn't want to lose it now. Some of the study had been fun, but some of it was unpleasant. Like dissecting dead bodies without wearing gloves. He was through that now, and he was learning about the important stuff—treating real patients.

He was especially inspired by his tutors who worked in research, in particular, Les Lazarus. Les used his scientific research to help his patients, which was known as 'bench to bedside' work.

Les was a striking man with a big black beard beginning to turn grey, and a brilliant scientific mind. He was different from the other doctors who taught at the university. They seemed remote and aloof, arriving on campus in big cars and wearing fancy suits. Les strode into tutorials wearing a white lab coat, looking as if he'd come from saving someone's life or making a scientific breakthrough.

Les was an endocrinologist, which meant he treated problems related to hormones, which are incredibly important for human health and development. **Endocrinology** also involved a lot of chemistry, a subject Cres loved.

As well as treating patients, Les had a research lab which Cres had visited. Recently, Les had invited Cres to do a research project with him on how sleep affected human growth hormones. This would mean taking a break from medical training for a year of experiments in the lab.

It sounded amazing to Cres, but when he'd mentioned to his mother that he was thinking of taking a year off for research at the end of semester, she'd said, 'Haven't you been at university long enough?' She had expected him to get a job as a respectable country doctor as soon as he could. When he started his medical degree, Cres had wanted this too, but lately he wasn't sure.

There was still so much to learn. He wanted to keep studying.

If they let him. If he hadn't ruined everything.

The next day, Cres was back at the hospital. The Director of Anaesthetics walked towards him, holding his clipboard.

'Good morning, Eastman,' he said.

'Good morning,' said Cres. He expected to be told off, or given an official warning, but nothing happened. It was as if Cres had never refused to follow the senior doctor's instructions.

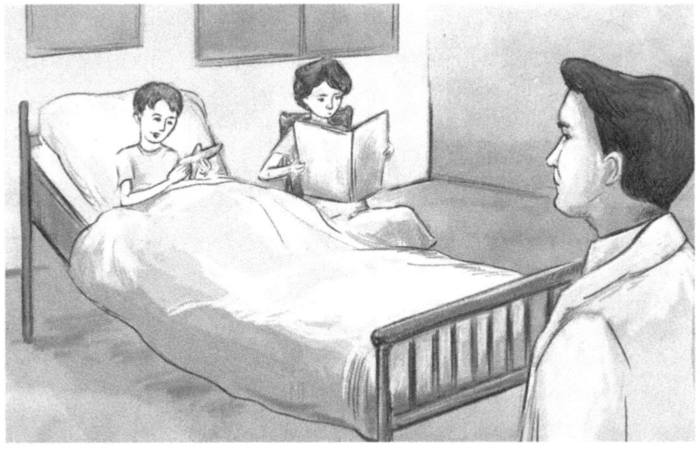

Later in the day, Cres visited the boy who'd had his tonsils out. He was sitting up in bed, playing with a toy plane while his mother sat beside him, reading a magazine. If the boy had been given the ether anaesthetic, he would still be feeling very unwell. Cres had taken a risk, but it had paid off for his patient.

*

Cres had shown he could learn independently, but the scholarships, mentoring and teaching he received during his medical degree allowed him to excel and become one of their strongest students. He qualified as a doctor, graduating with first place in the Medicine and Surgery examinations from St Vincent's Clinical School.

Cres completed a research project with Les Lazarus. He then went on to obtain Membership of the Royal Australasian College of Physicians, which granted him qualification as a Specialist Physician. After this, he was ready to begin the next stage of his career specialising in endocrinology.

8

London

In 1971 Cres moved to London after he was granted a prestigious Travelling Fellowship of the Royal Australasian College of Physicians. He received this partly due to glowing recommendations from Les Lazarus.

One lunchtime Cres sat at a white laminated table in the busy Middlesex Hospital canteen next to his new colleague, Jo Corcoran.

At the next table, a group of nurses sat talking and bursting into laughter occasionally.

The room smelled unappealingly of overcooked vegetables, but Cres had brought lunch from home.

'How are the kids?' asked Jo.

'Good,' said Cres, swallowing a bite of his sandwich. 'They've settled in well. Kate started preschool last week.'

'And Annette's home with the little ones?'

'That's right, Damien and Phillipa.'

'Has it been hard for Annette moving here?'

'Well, you know, Annette's very resilient,' said Cres. He felt a little defensive. Cres had one of the best paid fellowships, but even so, with three children money was tight. Some people might question why he'd dragged his family halfway across the world for a salary only a fraction of what he'd earn as a GP in Australia.

Luckily, Annette and the kids thought London was an exciting adventure. They'd seen Big Ben, the Tower of London and visited the British Museum.

History was everywhere in London, including at his work. The Middlesex Hospital was built in 1757. The entrance was an imposing U-shaped façade made of stone and brick. The hospital wards and laboratories were modern and fitted with shiny floors and new equipment. Even so, features like deeply set windows showed the old building's structure and solidness and reminded him that it had a long history.

He'd finished eating and asked Jo, 'You ready?'

They never took long for lunch. John Nabarro, their research leader, expected them to work long hours in the lab.

Jo nodded and stood up, saying, 'Back to it.'

She didn't sound enthusiastic, and Cres understood. Research could be exhilarating, but at times it was grinding and disappointing. This was one of those times.

Cres and Jo were trying to come up with a new method to measure thyroid hormones. These hormones, known as T3 and T4, are produced by the thyroid gland in humans and are important for growth, development, and for how the body converts food and drink into energy.

Specifically, Cres and Jo were developing a test to measure T3 in blood samples. This was difficult because the amount of T3 in blood is miniscule. A cup of blood on average contains only 0.5 micrograms of T3, which is half a millionth of a gram. However, a tiny change in the concentration of T3 in the blood could make a big difference to a person's health. If a person has too little or too much thyroid hormone, they could become sick, and even die.

The tests available in the 1970s weren't sensitive enough to measure these small differences, so John Nabarro's research group was developing a new method. The plan was to produce **antibodies** for T3. These antibodies would bind to T3 when added to a patient's blood sample.

> **Antibodie**s are Y-shaped molecules with sites that lock on or bind to substances such as bacteria, viruses, or hormones.

The leftover unbound antibodies could then be measured using a technique that was easier than measuring T3 itself. From this, the original amount of T3 could be calculated: The less unbound antibody left, the higher the concentration of T3.

It was like calculating how many seats were in a game of musical chairs by counting how many children were left standing at the end. If 10 children started the game, and 2 were standing at the end, it meant there were 8 chairs.

That was the idea, but it was easier said than done. For one thing, T3 could bind to a different molecule instead of the antibody. Like if some children sat on cushions instead of chairs when the music stopped.

Working out how to prevent this involved a lot of trial and error, and they needed a lot of antibodies.

To get the antibodies they injected Guinea pigs with thyroid hormone, which made the animals produce antibodies. These could then be harvested from the animals' blood.

It made Cres sad to see the small, caged Guinea pigs living restricted and lonely lives, and in any case they weren't the best animals to use in their experiments.

'The trouble is,' said Cres glumly as he pushed the lab door open. 'There isn't enough blood in Guinea pigs.'

'That's right,' agreed Jo, sitting at a stool in front of a microscope.

'We need bigger animals.'

'I suppose in Australia you'd use kangaroos,' Jo said, with a laugh.

Cres smiled. Everyone he met in England seemed to be obsessed with Australian wildlife. They imagined Australians had wallabies for pets and koalas living in the attic.

'Not kangaroos,' said Cres suddenly. 'Sheep. We'd use sheep.'

Jo laughed again, but Cres was serious. Why shouldn't they use sheep?

Initially John Nabarro, thought it was silly, but Cres convinced him to let them try. Jo and Cres established a new procedure. They would visit a farm in Redding and inject sheep with thyroid hormone along with other chemicals that caused an immune response in the animals, making them produce thyroid antibodies.

Ten weeks later, they returned to take blood. The sheep were lined up, as if they were about to be shorn, then the scientists painlessly took blood from a vein in the animals' necks. Afterwards the sheep got on with eating grass in the paddock.

This solved two problems: the sheep were happier than the Guinea pigs and the research team obtained larger quantities of antibodies.

After a day taking blood from sheep in the English countryside, they would stop at a country pub for a drink.

Then they'd return to London for the hard work in the lab. There were a lot of steps involved, and setbacks along the way, but eventually they developed a new testing procedure for T3 and also for the thyroid hormone T4.

They tested it out on patients at Middlesex Hospital and proved the test could accurately measure very small amounts of T3 and T4 in blood samples. This was a big scientific breakthrough that could help diagnose thyroid problems in patients.

Word of the new test got out and Cres and Jo received many requests for blood tests. One of these came from a well-respected Australian scientist, Basil Hetzel, who was studying how a lack of iodine caused thyroid conditions. Cres tested blood samples that Hetzel had collected in Papua New Guinea. It was interesting research and Cres was pleased his work could help.

Cres became even more interested in iodine and thyroid conditions after going to a conference in New Zealand. The world's experts were there, including Basil Hetzel. Listening to them talk, Cres realised that these scientists, who he respected and admired, actually didn't know the answers to many basic questions about thyroid hormones, iodine and how these affected the development of the human brain. He realised there was a lot to learn and that made it exciting. Answering these questions would become the major quest of Cres's scientific life.

*

One day after work, Cres was changing a lightbulb in their London flat when he heard the phone ring. He went to the hallway and picked up the cream handset.

'Creswell Eastman, speaking.'

He heard the slight pause that told him it was a long-distance call.

He repeated, 'Creswell Eastman.'

'Hi Cres, it's me.'

'Hello!' he said, surprised to hear from his sister. International calls were expensive in those days and were saved for special occasions, or emergencies.

Annette came into the room, a quizzical expression on her face.

'It's Margaret,' Cres mouthed.

'I'm sorry, I'm not calling with good news,' said Margaret. 'It's Mum.'

Cres suddenly felt clammy. He feared what she would say next.

'She's fading,' said Margaret. 'I think you should come home.'

*

Cres stood in line, waiting to board the plane for the long journey from London to Australia. It would include two stops, in Bahrain and Singapore, and take about 26 hours to get to Sydney. Then he would have to travel up to Lismore. He hoped he'd get there in time.

The flight attendant, wearing a small royal blue hat with a central red stripe, checked his boarding pass.

'Row 21, left-hand side, by the window, sir.'

He stepped into the plane's narrow corridor. It was a Boeing 747 and still had a new-furniture smell. The interior walls were lined with light yellow wallpaper with a wavy pattern. Each row of seats was a different colour. The effect was striking.

Cres found his seat and strapped his seatbelt on. He'd brought scientific articles to read, but for now he was happy to watch the planes out the window. It was a good distraction from his worried thoughts.

In the distance, another 747 was gathering speed. It reminded Cres of watching planes at the Evans Head aerodrome. These planes were so much bigger, though. Despite having studied physics, it still amazed Cres to see the heavy machines lift into the air.

The floor reverberated under his feet as the plane made its way towards the runway. After a brief pause, Cres heard and felt the engines churn to life, then the plane started to move again, speeding up quickly, pulling him backwards into his padded seat like an invisible hand. He felt a moment of apprehension and excitement. Then they were in the air, flying.

He watched the tiny rows of London houses below, remembering another trip home—catching a steam train back to Lismore when his father was dying. Nearly 20 years later, he was again travelling to Lismore to visit a dying parent, but in a jet plane. He'd come so far, but he still felt scared and sad. He was an adult, but he didn't want to be an orphan, he wasn't ready.

The plane was above the clouds now. He looked out the window, his eyes stinging from the brightness of the white clouds below.

*

A week later Cres sat by his mother's hospital bed. On her bedside table a vase held pink roses beside a statue of Mary. Meg's lunch sat on a tray in front of her, almost untouched. He didn't blame her; the smell was unappetising.

Since arriving in Australia, Cres had visited Meg several times, and spoken to her doctors and his sisters. He'd developed a theory that Meg had a thyroid condition that was causing her to be very sick.

'Have you thought about what I said yesterday?' he asked his mother.

'There's no point doing tests,' said Meg. 'The doctors say it's my heart, and there's nothing they can do.'

'I'm a doctor, too.'

'I thought you worked in a laboratory.'

'You can do both,' Cres replied. 'I see patients too. A blood test might give us the answers.' He was talking about the T3 test that he'd developed in London.

'Why didn't the other doctors suggest it?'

'They don't know about it yet.'

Meg nodded. 'Well, I suppose so. Could you hand me my rosary beads?' she asked.

A week later, Cres had his mother's results from the T3 test. They confirmed his suspicions. His mother had severe hypothyroidism, which meant her body wasn't producing enough thyroid hormone to function normally. This had led to her symptoms of heart failure, low body temperature, confusion, fluid retention and immobility.

The good news was that this condition could be treated with thyroid replacement hormones. Left untreated, she would die.

Cres explained the diagnosis and treatment to his mother.

'So, will this medicine work?' asked Meg.

'It'll take time, but yes, I expect it will.'

'So I'll be able to go home and live by myself?'

'Yes, I think so.'

Meg was silent for a few moments. Then she took his hand and squeezed it.

'You've done well,' she said. 'Thank you.'

As he left the hospital that day, Cres felt better than he had for a long time. It was exciting to understand a new area of medicine, but seeing his research help someone he cared about was an incredible reward. Even better, his mother understood why his work was important and was proud of him. He felt as if he'd graduated from medicine a second time.

*

Cres flew back to London and completed his fellowship.

Then Cres and his family returned to Australia to live. He took a job as Deputy Director of the **Garvan Institute** under his first mentor in medical research, Les Lazarus. This allowed him to work as a clinical scientist, continuing his scientific research and using the evidence-based results to treat his patients.

The **Garvan Institute** is a biomedical research institute founded in the 1960s as part of St Vincent's Hospital in Sydney. It is now one of Australia's largest and most respected medical research institutes.

The Garvan Institute received funding from a US company to prepare the technology Cres and Jo had worked on in London for world-wide use. Cres was very pleased to see how his research was helping so many people all over the world.

Two years later Cres decided to take a clinical job in Canberra at the Woden Valley and Canberra hospitals with a research appointment at the Australian National University. Some people were shocked that he was leaving Sydney and his job at the Garvan Institute where he had made friends and important work connections. Cres hadn't started with these but had gained success through hard work. The medical establishment had given him their blessing and then he seemed to have rejected it. Some people thought he was being ungrateful.

Ignoring warnings he was making a mistake, Cres knew he had to forge his own direction as a clinical scientist. He'd learned that sometimes you had to disappoint people and take the consequences. Cres's research team moved with him to Canberra.

Jo Corcoran came to Canberra too, and they continued their research using sheep on a farm near Goulburn to produce thyroid antibodies.

Cres always marvelled at the sheep's tolerance, standing patiently in the freezing cold wind while he and Jo took the blood they needed for their research.

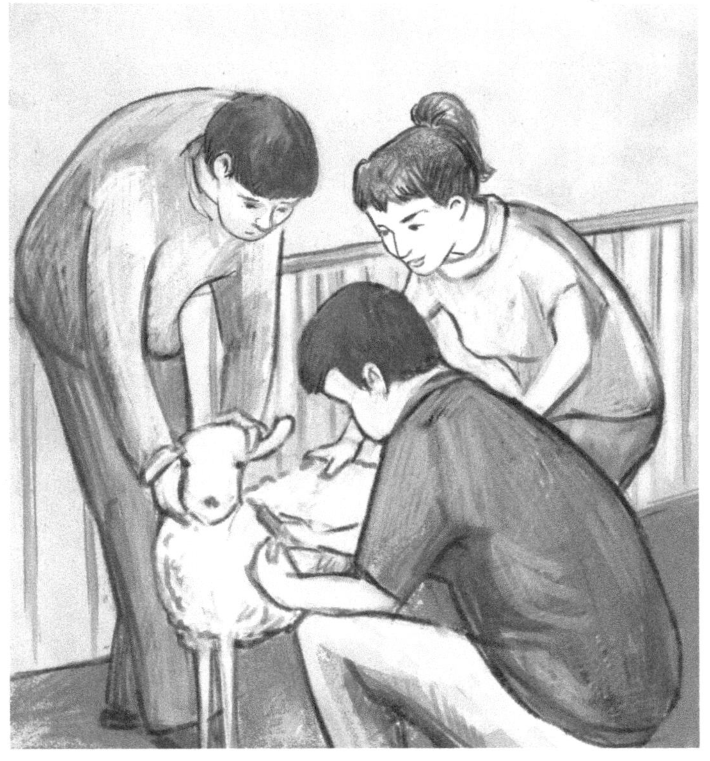

Through this process they developed an extremely sensitive test for thyroid hormones that meant newborn babies could be screened for thyroid disorders using only a tiny sample of blood.

This was really important because babies born with thyroid conditions could go on to develop intellectual and physical disabilities. The screening program for babies meant that thyroid problems could be picked up early and treated. Even so, some people opposed the new test, saying it was too difficult and expensive. Despite the opposition, Cres didn't give up, and in 1977 introduced a program to test all newborn babies for thyroid disorders in Canberra and surrounding hospitals in New South Wales. This soon became a standard test offered to all newborns in Australia.

Cres stayed in Canberra for four years, but then he received an offer he couldn't refuse. A new hospital was being built in Sydney called Westmead and they wanted him to be Head of Endocrinology. Cres's family and his research group moved back to Sydney and the next part of his career began.

9

Sarawak

When Cres was working at the Garvan Institute, a student called Glen Maberly came to speak with him. Glen asked Cres to help with his research project on goitres in people in Sarawak, a remote part of Malaysia.

Cres was fascinated with this work so agreed to help.

Goitres are swellings in the thyroid gland in the neck. They may be small and barely noticeable but can grow to the size of melons and be very uncomfortable. They often occur in people who lack iodine in their diets. Iodine is one of the building blocks of thyroid hormones T3 and T4. If someone doesn't have enough iodine to make these hormones the thyroid gland works harder to produce them. This makes the thyroid gland swell and get bigger, becoming a goitre.

The amount of iodine a person needs over their whole lifetime would fit in a teaspoon, but they need this in regular small doses. Sometimes people's diets contain enough iodine. Seafood, seaweed, milk and vegetables grown in iodine-rich soils are great sources of iodine.

In inland and mountainous regions, iodine leaches from the soil over time when it rains, flowing into rivers and out to sea. As a result, people living far from the ocean often don't get enough iodine from their diets.

Goitres are one symptom of iodine deficiency and thyroid problems, but there are others. During Cres's career, researchers discovered how essential thyroid hormones are to human health from before birth, to the end of life.

*

The long, narrow boat rocked as Cres stepped into it. He sat on the wooden bench, relieved he hadn't fallen in, gripping his backpack between his knees.

His whole body felt wet with sweat, not from exercise but from the hot steamy air.

There were no roads for vehicles through the dense tropical jungle. To get to remote Malaysian villages in Sarawak you needed to travel by riverboat.

Glen was already sitting in the boat, looking comfortable. He turned around and smiled. Cres gave him a thumbs up. Glen had travelled to Sarawak many times before. His brother and father worked as **missionaries** there so had helped arrange transport and places to stay.

A missionary is a member of a religious group sent to an area to promote their faith to people who aren't members of that religion.

Cres felt lucky to be in the boat today. There had been heavy rain recently, but the river had gone down enough to allow safe travel.

On this trip Glen and Cres were planning to measure the goitre size and iodine levels of people in the local community. Then they would install an iodinator, which would add iodine to the water supply. Nine months later they would return to measure goitres and iodine levels again. These would be compared to a village with no iodinator to assess whether it was effective.

Sitting in the narrow boat, Cres gazed at the dark green jungle on the opposite bank. The foliage came to the edge of the swirling, muddy brown Lemanak River.

The boat's outboard motor roared to life and Cres felt the vessel juddering beneath him, smelling the pungent burning diesel fumes.

During the two-hour journey the river twisted in front of them. After every bend, another stretch of brown river and dense jungle appeared. Large trees grew close to the banks, the trunks wrapped with ferns and brightly coloured flowers. Sometimes they passed through a tunnel of greenery where the jungle canopy closed over the river.

This was a big change from Cres's life in Sydney. Much of his work happened at a new, bright, bustling city hospital. As head of the Endocrine Unit at Westmead Hospital, Cres had a busy schedule seeing patients, supervising research and doing paperwork. It couldn't be a bigger contrast to sitting in a small boat on a jungle river. It almost felt like a dream, except the hard wooden seat, humidity and itchy bites were very real.

Eventually, Cres heard the boat's pilot call out, pointing towards a landing on the shore. They'd arrived.

Cres was relieved to step onto solid ground. Well, sort of solid—the ground was muddy and squished beneath his feet.

Cres smiled and nodded to the people from the village who had come to welcome them. Cres always noticed people's necks, so he saw that many of the people had large goitres just as Glen had reported.

Standing out amongst the group was a tall blonde man, who introduced himself as Sven Hansen. He was from the engineering company that had donated the iodinators for the project.

Cres smiled warmly at Sven who was looking worried.

'We have a problem,' Sven said, after they exchanged greetings. 'The headman won't let us install the iodinators.'

The headman, known as Tuai Rumah, was similar to a mayor and was elected by the people. It was essential to gain his approval for any project.

'What do you mean?' said Glen.

'He's worried that the iodine is poison,' explained Sven. 'He's heard about bad experiences after iodine injections in another village. I told him he's wrong.'

'He's not wrong exactly,' said Cres. 'Iodine injections did cause side effects. That's why we want to try the iodinators.' Their theory was that a low, steady dose of iodine might be better than an injection.

Cres knew people were desperate to cure uncomfortable goitres. Sometimes they tried dangerous surgery, like cutting open the neck to remove a goitre. But Cres also understood why the headman worried that the treatment might make goitres worse. The headman was making decisions that would affect people's health—he was responsible to his community.

Sven shrugged.

'I've tried to explain,' he said. 'Maybe he'll listen to you.'

Ahead, Cres could see the longhouse where they would stay. It was an impressive structure, elevated three metres above the ground on stilts. Pigs snuffled in the black mud underneath, alongside chickens scratching for grubs.

He followed Glen up the carved wooden steps onto the uncovered platform. The floor was made of slats to let cool air come up into the building. This also allowed food scraps to fall below for the animals to eat. Cres could see through the slats to the ground metres below. Luckily, he wasn't bothered by heights.

Beyond the platform was a wide verandah in front of the building's enclosed section. There were dozens of doors along the verandah, which led into the common room and family rooms. The common room was a big space where people worked, ate, and danced. Each family also had a separate room to themselves.

It was very different from Australian homes, where most people lived with their immediate family members in separate houses or apartments. Here, more space was shared, and people mixed together more often. Families in the longhouse looked after each other's children and helped each other with daily tasks.

Beside each door was a rooster in a cage. These were valuable birds, bred and trained for cockfighting. Cres also noticed blackened balls, like oddly shaped coconuts, hanging from the rafters. They were shrunken human heads, reminders of the community's past as head-hunters.

From inside the building, Cres heard a radio blaring an advertisement for Coca-Cola. You couldn't get away from advertising anywhere it seemed.

The headman greeted them on the verandah. He wore black shorts and a light-blue collared shirt and despite Sven's report, he seemed friendly and happy to see them. They sat down with the headman to drink tea that was sickly sweet with a lot of local palm sugar added. Cres found it too sweet, but he drank it anyway to be polite.

The scientists discussed the project with the headman, with a guide translating for them. The headman explained he was worried the iodinators would make goitres worse. Cres explained what the benefits could be. The headman promised to talk with the community and consider it.

Later that evening Cres lay on his air mattress under a mosquito net on the verandah, exhausted but not able to sleep. He was uncomfortable and suspected his mattress had a slow leak. He was also worried about the project.

That evening the community had welcomed them very warmly. They'd eaten together, sitting on the floor in a circle in the community room with the food in the middle. After dinner there was lots of dancing. Despite this generous hospitality, it seemed the trip could easily fail. If the headman decided not to let them install the iodinator, many people would keep suffering from iodine deficiency and the illnesses that came from that.

Cres tried to stop worrying by focusing on the sounds around him. The night was surprisingly loud. The high canopy of leaves rustled in the wind and there was a constant harmony of frog and bird calls. Closer by, pigs grunted under the longhouse and occasionally a dog barked. Eventually, Cres's body relaxed, his breathing slowed and he drifted to sleep.

He was woken by a rooster crowing, seemingly right next to his head. It was still dark, so Cres shut his eyes, hoping to sleep again. Another rooster crowed, and then another. The caged birds seemed to be competing for the loudest crow, and the competition was fierce.

The human noises around the longhouse increased too. Footsteps pounded along the bamboo floor and Cres felt the reverberations through the slats pressing into his back because his air mattress was now completely flat. Shouts and laughter floated up from near the river.

Cres felt as if he'd barely slept. I'll need a lot of coffee today, he thought. Then he remembered there probably wouldn't be coffee. It would be a long day.

There was a sound closer by. Footsteps on the porch beside him. A small voice spoke, 'Doctor Eastman. My brother is sick. Will you come?'

Cres sat up and recognised the boy standing next to him as the headman's grandson. He was a clever boy who had learned English at boarding school.

Cres nodded and stood up. He picked up his medical bag and followed the boy into the longhouse where the morning light barely penetrated the gloom. By the light of a small lamp Cres saw an older boy lying under a blanket on a bed.

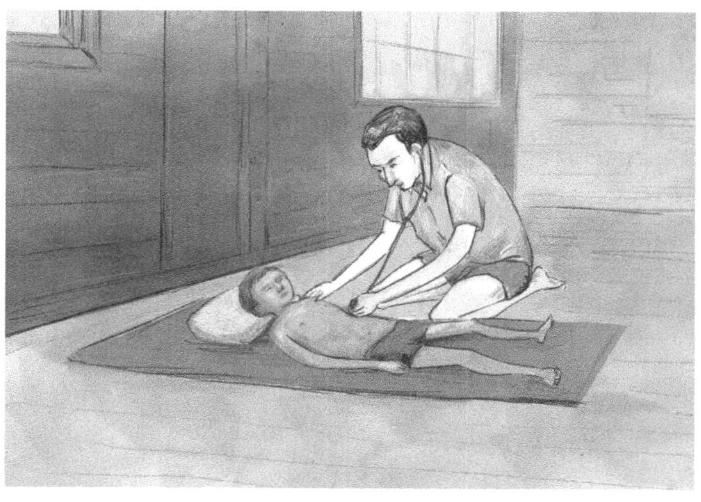

The headman sat beside his grandson. The man looked worried, and Cres recognised the feeling he'd experienced as a father. Seeing your child in pain was terrible.

'He's sick,' said the younger boy. 'Getting worse all night.'

Cres knelt down and examined the patient. The boy had a high fever. His breathing was laboured and even in the dim light, Cres could tell his skin was pale with a dark tinge around his lips. Cres listened to the boy's chest. He suspected pneumonia, inflamed lungs caused by an infection.

Using his younger grandson as a translator, Cres explained to the headman that he could give the boy **penicillin**. The medicine would be injected deep into the boy's muscles so it would be absorbed quickly into his bloodstream.

Penicillin was the first antibiotic used by doctors. It's produced naturally by certain blue moulds but is now usually prepared synthetically for medicine. Penicillin was discovered by Alexander Fleming in 1928 when he noticed that bacteria didn't grow in his petri dish where there was mould.

The headman agreed.

Cres's team had brought a well-stocked medical kit to treat themselves if they got sick, but also to help local people if they could. Cres prepared the medication and injected it into the boy's arm. He sat by the boy's bed throughout the day, monitoring his condition. By nightfall, he was doing better. His temperature was down, and his breathing steady. He even sat up and talked to his grandfather.

Pneumonia can kill people but antibiotics are a simple and effective treatment. Cres knew from his brother, Alistair, that antibiotics could be the difference between life and death.

The younger boy approached where Cres was sitting cross-legged on the floor and said, 'My grandfather says you can fix the water.'

Cres looked at the headman, who nodded at him.

Cres didn't speak the local language, but he knew the word for 'thank you'.

'*Terima kasih Aya Tuai Rumah!*'

The headman responded with a nod.

Cres had said he'd try to help, and he had been true to his word. That was essential to building trust. Consistency and honesty were critical.

The next day Sven, Cres and Glen worked with locals to dig trenches and install plumbing for the iodinator.

The water supply came from local streams, diverted to the longhouse. The water would pass through the iodinator, which contained iodine crystals. As the water flowed through, some iodine dissolved in the water.

Cres connected the pipes and installed the tap in the village. It was hard work in the hot, humid climate, and everyone ended up covered in black mud. But after a week they had something to show for their hard work. The longhouse had water containing iodine.

Cres showed the headman how to judge the concentration of iodine and how to adjust it. Water with too much iodine tastes like metal, and at even higher concentrations the water becomes yellow.

During their visit Cres and Glen also took blood and urine samples from community members and measured the number and size of goitres.

Nine months later, the research team returned to the village. There had been a significant decrease in goitres and size. No villagers reported negative effects. The iodine also sterilised the water so there had been fewer illnesses caused by contaminated drinking water. The headman was very happy and Cres was extremely pleased that the project had made such a big difference to people in the village.

The Malaysian government also took notice of the work and made changes throughout the region to ensure people got enough iodine. From one research project in a small and remote village Cres and his team improved the health of thousands of people.

This project in Sarawak was the start of Cres's international fieldwork that would eventually impact on millions of lives.

10

China

In 1982 Cres invited researchers from the Tianjin Medical College in China to an international thyroid conference in Tokyo, Japan. Cres was keen to encourage Chinese scientists to interact on the international stage. The Chinese researchers told Cres how common goitres were in China and said they wanted outside help with their research.

Cres received Australian funding to complete a project on iodine deficiency in China. He had no idea how this small research project would balloon into something much bigger.

One afternoon in the early 1980s, Cres arrived home in Sydney from Beijing. He was exhausted. He'd visited many Chinese villages, some in remote areas and was shocked by what he'd seen.

Despite how weary he felt that afternoon Cres still went to his son's cricket training as he was the assistant coach and went to as many sessions as he could. While the boys did catching drills Cres's eyes closed, he rocked forward on his toes and startled himself. His eyes snapped open.

'Good work!' he called out, hoping no one had noticed him fall asleep standing up.

After he and Nicholas got home from training, he gave his kids their gifts—small jade ornaments and painted fans. While they ate dinner Cres told them about his trip, highlighting the positives, including the beautiful views of emerald-green rice paddies and the wonderful food.

After dinner, Cres and Annette sat in the lounge room having a cup of tea. He told her the truth. 'It was terrible.'

'Why?' asked Annette.

'It's hard to describe,' he replied.

He told her about the same scene that was repeated in village after village. Walking along the dusty main street of a town, shaded by poplar trees, Cres had seen people standing in doorways or walking down the street, and quickly recognised their facial expressions, small bodies, and unusual walking style as signs of severe Iodine Deficiency Disorders. The symptoms included development delays, **cognitive impairment**, restricted growth, blindness, and hearing loss.

Cognitive impairment is when a person has trouble concentrating, remembering, learning new things, making decisions or solving problems.

It made life a lot harder, in many ways.

Severe Iodine Deficiency Disorders occur when children don't receive enough thyroid hormones before and just after being born. If it happens before they are born, the condition is irreversible. It can't be treated.

Thyroid hormones are essential for brain development. In the first few weeks of pregnancy, a pregnant person's body normally doubles their production of thyroid hormones to supply the baby in the womb.

Iodine is a building block of thyroid hormones, so pregnant people need more iodine. If a pregnant person doesn't get enough iodine, or if they have a damaged thyroid gland, they won't produce enough thyroid hormone for the baby to develop typically.

Because thyroid issues in pregnancy are urgent, Cres always saw these patients first, even before patients with cancer. Every day was precious and early treatment could greatly help the unborn child.

'It's so sad,' said Cres to Annette. 'People in villages try to look after each other, but it's hard when so many people have problems.'

'How many people does it affect?'

'A quarter of China's population have goitres. That's 300 million people. It's mind-boggling. And that means millions of people will also have brain damage.'

'Do we get enough iodine in Australia?'

'Yes. We get iodine from milk, actually,' said Cres. He tapped his cup of milky tea.

'Do cows have a lot of iodine?'

'No, but dairy farmers use iodine mixed with detergents as a disinfectant for milking equipment. Some iodine ends up in the milk.'

'So, the milk is contaminated?' asked Annette, looking down into her cup suspiciously.

'Yeah, but it's not a bad thing. It means that Australians get enough iodine, even if you didn't grow up near the sea like me. It's an accidental public health triumph.'

'What can be done in China?' asked Annette. 'Could they add iodine to the water like you did in Sarawak?'

'That can be expensive for large populations. But there are other solutions. Like adding iodine to salt.'

'Why don't they do that?'

'I don't know! It's frustrating.' Cres closed his eyes for a moment, suddenly feeling very tired.

'Why don't you do something about it?' said Annette.

Cres opened his eyes and saw Annette was sitting forward on her chair, looking excited by the idea.

'I don't have any experience in international public health,' said Cres slowly. 'I'd need funding.'

'You're great at getting grants.'

'That's medical research funding. This is something different. You've gotta apply to Australian international **aid** programs or something.'

'Why not? I'm sure it's the same. You just have to explain how your project will meet the program's aims.'

Aid is assistance given by one country to another. The aid could be money, goods or services.

After seeing the suffering in the villages Cres knew he had to try. He was a scientist, but he was a human being first. He couldn't walk past that kind of suffering.

Cres's research had helped explain how iodine deficiency caused problems for unborn children. It would lead to papers published in scientific journals, and more research funding. It could mean prestigious job offers and invitations to speak at medical conferences. But unless his work changed people's lives, Cres couldn't see the point.

He wrote an application explaining the benefits of reducing Iodine Deficiency Disorders, and how the project would help Australia's relationship with China.

His proposal was received politely. The government officials said it was interesting, and obviously a huge problem, but it wasn't something they could fund now. They would keep it on file.

Cres suspected the file would gather dust on someone's desk forever, but one way or another he was determined to make his research change people's lives.

*

A year later, Cres was running the weekly Diabetes Clinic at Westmead Hospital. It was always a long and busy day.

He was between patients when he heard a knock on his door.

'Come in!' said Cres.

A nurse opened the door and said, 'Dr Eastman, there's someone on the phone for you. He's from the Prime Minister's office.'

'I'm about to see a patient,' said Cres. 'But if he wants a clinic appointment, give him one.'

The nurse was back a minute later. 'I'm afraid he still wants to speak with you,' she said. 'It's not about an appointment.'

'Okay. Thanks,' said Cres. 'Put him through.' He hoped this wouldn't take too long—he had patients to see.

A moment later the phone rang, and Cres picked up. The person introduced himself as a senior adviser to the Prime Minister, Bob Hawke. He explained that Hawke would be visiting China the next week.

'The thing about these relationships is that you have to give as well as get,' explained the advisor. 'So, we'll be announcing Australian aid for a bridge and a forest. And we also want a health project.'

A flicker of excitement went through Cres. He'd submitted his Iodine Deficiency Disorders application ages ago and had assumed it had failed. Suddenly, there was hope!

The man continued, 'And we came across your project for iodine...deficiency...disorder.' Cres could tell the advisor was reading the unfamiliar term from a piece of paper. The man continued, 'So, can you come to Beijing on Monday?'

'What?!' said Cres, shocked at how fast the conversation was moving.

'We'd need you there for the announcement on Monday.'

'You don't understand,' said Cres. 'I'm a hospital specialist. I can't leave at a moment's notice. I have patients.'

'I see. We might have to look at other projects then—'

'No, no, don't do that,' said Cres. 'Let me get back to you.'

Cres felt shaken when he hung up the phone but he immediately called the hospital's General Superintendent and told him what had happened.

'He'll announce funding for other aid projects, but our project could be the health one. I've been invited so I can answer the medical questions,' explained Cres.

'You should be there,' said the Superintendent. 'It could boost Westmead's international reputation. Leave it with me.'

An hour later it was organised. Cres's patients at the hospital would be looked after by other specialists, the tickets and accommodation were booked and paid for. Cres was going to Beijing.

Cres sat at his desk dazed by how quickly the situation had developed. He wondered how he'd get along with Bob Hawke. For a start, although he didn't drink alcohol while prime minister, Bob Hawke held a world record for beer drinking and was reportedly an extravert who swore like a sailor. Whereas Cres was quiet and thought carefully before he spoke. They both loved sport though, so Cres supposed they could always talk about cricket.

Later in the day, as Cres left the clinic, he saw Mu Li in the corridor. She was a new research student and the first student from China to study at Westmead. She was an intelligent and enthusiastic student, joining journal clubs and coming on clinical rounds. To improve her English, she recorded tutorials then listened to them late into the evening.

He and Annette had invited Mu for dinner at their house. She got along well with their children and fitted in easily with the family.

'Good afternoon, Professor Eastman!' she said warmly. Mu was always pleased to see Cres. He reminded Mu of her father, a successful doctor in China.

'I'm glad I ran into you,' Cres said. 'I'm sorry but I'll have to cancel our meeting this week. You know what to keep working on?'

Mu nodded. 'Is everything okay?' she asked, looking worried.

'Yes, it's great. I just got news about the application for funding in China. I'm going to Beijing for the announcement, with the Prime Minister.'

'Congratulations, Professor Eastman!'

Cres continued, 'We'll have a meeting about this when I get back. You're going to be an important part of the team, Mu.'

Mu Li watched him walk away. She was excited to work on this project, Cres's enthusiasm was infectious. She didn't want to let him down.

Cres made lots of people feel that way—it was part of how he got so much done.

*

Six years later, it was 1993 when Cres arrived at the Diaoyutai State Guesthouse, where the Chinese government often held diplomatic meetings. The State Guesthouse was a grand complex of buildings and beautiful gardens. Diaoyutai meant 'fishing terrace' so there were tranquil lakes, and streams well-stocked with fish. Weeping willows lined the shores and elaborately decorated pavilions and stone bridges dotted the garden.

It was a tranquil scene, but Cres wasn't feeling calm.

Glen Maberly came and stood beside him. Glen's student days were long behind him, and he was now a successful doctor and independent researcher.

'We've come a long way from the jungles in Malaysia, hey?' said Glen as they looked across the lake.

Cres smiled. 'We have,' he agreed, but he thought there was also a long way to go. Their meeting today could determine the rest of the journey.

The past six years had built towards this moment. Since receiving funding from the Australian government, Cres and his team at Westmead Hospital had worked with Chinese doctors and officials to reduce iodine deficiency in China. They'd trained Chinese doctors and scientists and set up medical centres in remote areas to monitor people's iodine levels and treat thyroid conditions. They'd also made startling findings on how iodine deficiency affected people. He wanted to make sure this research would result in changes to improve people's health.

Cres had learned a lot about international diplomacy and public health. He'd built relationships with groups like the **World Health Organisation (WHO)**, **United Nations International Children's Emergency Fund (UNICEF)**, and the Chinese Ministry of Health.

The United Nations (UN) is an organisation made up of almost all the world's countries. **WHO** and **UNICEF** are branches of the UN. The WHO works on international public health. **UNICEF** tries to protect children's rights and ensure they have the opportunity to reach their full potential.

Although the program was a success, Cres knew they needed to speak directly to the decision-makers at the top of government. That was the way to make progress across the whole country.

That's why today's meeting was so important. He and a small delegation had come to the State Guest House to meet with Zhu Rongji, the Vice-Premier of China. Zhu Rongji was in charge of China's economic development program and was a key person to convince. They would tell him what their research had found, and what they recommended he should do to reduce iodine deficiency.

The delegation was taken to a three-storey building with a magnificent, yellow-glazed tile roof, green painted pillars and carved beams. Two gilded copper lions guarded the front gate and three red lanterns adorned the entrance.

Cres and the group walked through the golden doors and were directed to a waiting room.

Another group were already there. A man wearing a khaki suit and a black and white headdress was examining a painting. He was smoking a black cigarette and the terrible smell wafted through the room.

The man turned around and to his shock, Cres realised it was Yasser Arafat, the leader of the Palestine Liberation Organisation (PLO).

'Good morning,' Cres said.

'Good morning,' Yasser Arafat replied politely. 'Good weather.'

Cres agreed. He noticed the dark yellow staining on the man's fingers from holding his awful cigarettes. Cres had a strong urge to cough, but he fought it back.

He suddenly felt as if he was out of his body. He saw himself from above, in an opulent room, about to meet with the Vice-Premier of China and making small talk with a leader, who many in the Western world considered infamous. What would his mother have thought?

Yasser Arafat returned to his group, and the only sound in the room was the men talking amongst themselves in Arabic.

After a few moments, a set of large doors opened, and the Australian delegation was taken into the meeting room where Vice-Premier Zhu Rongji was waiting. He wore a dark suit and had thick, perfectly styled black hair.

After the initial greetings, Cres began his presentation. It was different from the usual talks Cres made about his scientific research. He wasn't just presenting evidence and theories; he was making an argument about what the Chinese government should do. Zhu Rongji needed to understand the impact of Iodine Deficiency Disorders, but more importantly, to act to prevent them.

Cres told the Vice-Premier what they'd learned in China:

- 700 million people lived in iodine-deficient areas.
- 400 million Chinese people were directly affected by Iodine Deficiency Disorders.
- 250,000 Chinese people had severe brain damage because of Iodine Deficiency Disorders.

'Recently, we've made an even more important finding,' said Cres. 'Children living in areas with mild iodine deficiency show an average reduction in IQ of 10 to 15 points.'

Cres paused and glanced at Zhu Rongji, but he couldn't gauge the man's reaction.

Cres continued, 'Children with mild iodine deficiency don't always show obvious signs of disorders, but they still have reduced capacity on average. This means their educational and economic opportunities are reduced.'

As a doctor, Cres's main concern was people's health and wellbeing. But to convince governments to act he needed to emphasise how the problem affected economic growth.

Cres said, 'The impact on the economy when so many people can't contribute fully is enormous.'

Zhu Rongji nodded seriously, then asked, 'Why haven't I heard this before?'

'Previously, people thought iodine deficiency just caused goitres,' explained Cres. 'Now we know it's more than that. Goitres are the smoke that warns us of a fire. In this case, the fire is brain damage.'

'What can be done?' asked Zhu Rongji.

Cres was prepared. They couldn't just present the problem. They had to provide a solution.

'Iodised salt,' he replied. 'Everyone needs salt, and it's cheap to add iodine without changing the flavour. This has been tried here in China, but there are thousands of salt producers. It needs to be made **mandatory**, or it won't work. The salt also needs to be monitored. Government regulation could make this happen.'

Cres was aware that their time with the Vice-Premier was coming to an end. Although he seemed engaged and interested, the leader hadn't committed to anything.

Zhu Rongji was about to speak. Cres leant forward in his chair.

The Vice-Premier finally said, 'I will make sure it is done.'

Cres felt a surge of excitement and triumph. He couldn't wait to tell Mu Li and the Westmead team! He wished he could celebrate as if he'd kicked a goal. But running around hugging people and jumping in the air wouldn't have been appropriate. He kept his excitement inside. Glen and Cres managed to smile across at each other before thanking the Vice Premier for meeting with them.

This meeting was a turning point for Iodine Deficiency Disorders in China. The Chinese government made it illegal to sell non-iodised salt for humans to eat.

Cres wanted to ensure that iodine deficiency elimination efforts would continue even when the Australian researchers were no longer involved. With this in mind, Cres, Mu Li and Gary Ma raised one million dollars through AusAID to set up the National Reference Laboratory Monitoring and Training Centre in Beijing. This institution monitored the iodisation program and trained Chinese scientists to continue this work.

Monitoring included surveys every two to five years. Previously, only 40% of Chinese households used iodised salt. This rose to 90% after the laws were introduced. More importantly, monitoring showed that iodine levels in children rose, goitres reduced, and babies stopped being born with severe Iodine Deficiency Disorders.

It's hard to measure the total impact of these changes, but they improved the health and lives of millions of Chinese people.

11

Tibet

The plane hit the ground with a satisfying smoothness. Cres thought it was his best landing yet.

'Good work,' said Cres's flying instructor. Arthur Caruana was seated at the controls next to Cres, a reassuring, steady presence. Arthur had short dark hair and a friendly face. Usually, these days Cres was the teacher, but at flight school he became the student. Cres didn't mind. He always wanted to learn new things.

'Now, turn around and taxi back, please,' said Arthur.

Cres followed the instructions. Then Arthur unbuckled his seatbelt. He opened the door to step out. Cres was confused because the lesson wasn't over yet.

'You're on your own,' said Arthur. 'Go and do one touch and go, land, and then pick me up again.'

Cres had known this was coming. If it wasn't this week, it would have been next week, or the week after that. Yet he was still shocked that he was going to fly a plane solo.

He'd waited a long time for this. Watching the planes in Evans Head, nine-year old Cres had been certain he would become a pilot. As he'd got older, Cres hadn't always been sure. He first had flying lessons while living in Canberra. He'd ending up quitting though. Flying light aircraft could be dangerous and he'd been persuaded that the risks were too great for someone with four young children.

Twenty years later, Cres was in his fifties, and his children were adults, studying at university or starting their own careers. This was his moment.

Cres's stomach felt queasy with nerves as he completed his checks before take-off. The tasks gave him something to focus on. When his brain was occupied, he didn't notice his body as much.

During take-off Cres paid close attention to monitoring the plane's controls. He didn't have time to consider how he felt.

Once in the air, he glanced at the empty seat beside him. It hit him that he was alone in the sky. He was the only one who could bring the plane safely back to earth.

Cres flew a circuit around the aerodrome and completed Arthur's instructions.

Everything went smoothly and when he picked up Arthur, Cres was grinning. He'd survived his first solo flight. Although Cres had reached a lot of academic goals in his life, qualifying as a doctor, completing a higher degree in medicine, finishing a Leadership and Management program at Harvard University, none of these achievements could beat the feeling of learning to fly.

'You never forget your first solo flight,' said Arthur.

Cres grinned. He was sure he wouldn't.

He learned to fly for his own enjoyment, but he also used his pilot's licence for work. When his team needed to visit regional communities, Cres could fly them himself, which saved a lot of time and money.

It took longer than he'd expected but his first dream to become a pilot came true.

*

By the late 1990s, it was clear that some areas in China were lagging in getting rid of Iodine Deficiency Disorders. For example, in Tibet goitres were still common and lots of Tibetan children were born with brain damage due to their mothers' iodine deficient diets.

The Chinese government was impressed with Cres's work so suggested that Cres and his team complete a survey to find out how bad the problem was in Tibet and then come up with a solution.

In 1999 Cres was on a Chinese military aeroplane flying into a remote area of Tibet. They would land at the **highest altitude airport** in the world, Qamdo Bamda, over 4,000 metres above sea level.

The **highest altitude airport** in the world is now Daocheng Yading Airport in Tibet, which opened in 2013. It is 4,411 metres above sea level, twice as high as Australia's highest mountain—Mt Kosciuszko.

As a pilot and lover of planes, Cres was excited to arrive at this unique airport. Initially, Cres had expected to travel by land, but this chartered flight saved days of travel, so more time to visit villages and collect information.

He looked out the plane window at the brown mountains topped with snow, a blue river winding like a ribbon between them.

Through the crackly speakers, the pilot made an announcement in Mandarin.

Cres's guide leaned over and translated, 'Landing soon, Professor Eastman.'

'Thanks, Wang.'

Cres marvelled at the 5.5-kilometre runway as they landed. It was the longest runway in the world because planes need longer to speed up at high altitude with the air being less dense.

After the plane taxied back to the terminal, Cres picked up his bag and made his way to the plane's exit, noticing the flight crew were wearing oxygen masks. Cres was uneasy but tried to sound cheerful as he said goodbye to the crew.

After only a few metres walking across the tarmac towards the airport terminal, Cres felt breathless. He put down his bag and took a few deep breathes. At high altitude, the air contains less oxygen, but Cres hadn't expected it would affect him this much.

He was also still recovering from a stomach bug he'd picked up a few days before. He was dehydrated and could feel a headache starting.

He suddenly remembered what the Director General of Health for Tibet had said to him in a recent meeting: 'You've done remarkable things, Professor Eastman. But this is going to be the most difficult project you've taken on. This will threaten your life.'

Cres had thought the man was exaggerating or trying to put him off. Now his warning seemed too real. Had he made a big mistake?

Travelling by car to their accommodation, Cres felt worse. His head was aching and breathing was difficult, even though he was sitting still.

When they arrived, Cres set himself up with an oxygen mask. It was Mother's Day in Australia, so he called Annette by satellite phone. She sounded very far away.

'You're a wonderful mother,' Cres said, 'and the most resilient person I know.'

He wanted to say more, but he was struggling for breath.

'Are you sure you're okay?' Annette asked.

He explained he was sick but tried to be reassuring.

'I'll be better in the morning.'

He hung up, feeling further away from his family than ever before.

By nightfall Cres had a bubbling sensation in his chest, which he knew meant fluid was coming from his blood vessels into his airways. Even worse, he suspected fluid was building up around his brain. His headache was the worst he'd ever had, as if hundreds of sharp knives were pressing against his skull.

It was hard to think clearly, but he had to. He was the team leader but also the only doctor, and they were hundreds of kilometres from the nearest hospital. No one was coming to save him. If he was going to live, he had to save himself.

First, Cres inserted a catheter into his arm so he could inject medication directly into his veins. Then he gave himself a high dose of a steroid called dexamethasone that would hopefully reduce inflammation. He took another medication to reduce the fluid in his body. And he kept wearing an oxygen mask.

Even with these treatments he knew his body would struggle to recover at high altitude. He spoke to Wang and said, 'First light, you've gotta get me into a vehicle. Pack up everything here, get my equipment and gear. You've gotta get me to a lower altitude.'

Wang's sombre face told Cres he must look as sick as his felt.

That night, Cres slept in small bursts, often waking in intense pain. The medication he'd taken also made him need to go to the toilet often. But he couldn't walk to the bathroom, so he urinated into an empty, plastic water bottle.

He woke again and this time he heard bustling footsteps as people busily packed up the car. He opened his eyes to grey morning light coming through the window. He turned his head and saw the bottle he'd used the night before. The liquid inside was a dusky dark shade, like red wine.

This colour happened when red blood cells were destroyed and passed out in urine. It was another sign that he was extremely sick.

Cres felt a little better, but when he sat up, his head felt fuzzy. At least his headache wasn't as bad.

Wang came in bringing a bowl of cereal. Cres managed to eat only a few spoonfuls. Wang offered him a cup of instant coffee. Cres shook his head.

With Wang's help, Cres stood up and walked to the 4-wheel-drive vehicle where he sat in the back with Wang beside him.

The engine started and the car bumped along the rocky driveway. While the movement hurt Cres's head, he was glad to be underway.

They drove out of the village and onto a narrow dirt road down the mountain, travelling along twisting roads dangerously close to sharp cliff edges. One wrong move and the car would plunge them to their deaths. Luckily, Cres trusted the local drivers who had driven these roads many times before.

'Professor Eastman,' said Wang. Cres saw that Wang was holding the bottle of red urine from the night before. Wang thrust it towards Cres and said, 'Take your medicine.'

'That's not medicine!' protested Cres.

'Yes!' said Wang. 'You drank this last night, and today you are much better. You must have more medicine.'

Cres tried to explain, 'It's urine.'

Wang looked confused.

'Wee,' tried Cres.

Wang still didn't understand. Cres tried to say the word in Mandarin, but Wang looked even more confused.

'You must have your medicine,' Wang insisted taking off the cap and trying to press the bottle into Cres's hand.

'It's piss!' said Cres.

'Piss!' said Wang, with a look of surprised understanding. He stared at the bottle in amazement.

Wang asked the driver to stop the car then opened the door and stepped out. Yaks grazed in the distance, a familiar sight in Tibet. Wang started to pour, and Cres saw the red fluid gushing out onto the grass.

Wang turned and said with a smile, 'Professor Eastman, you are a strong man, so this will be good for the yaks.'

Despite his headache, Cres smiled. He would tell this story to many people, how his guide had nearly made him drink his own urine, and then told him it would make the yaks stronger. It was a light-hearted end to the story of how he nearly died on a Tibetan mountain.

It took Cres six months to recover from his illness. He had learned valuable lessons: always travel slowly to high altitudes and never travel to a remote location without another doctor on the team.

*

Cres continued to work in Tibet, even after his serious illness on the mountain. The information he gathered showed most people weren't getting enough iodine. As a result, goitres were common. More importantly, in some areas 13% of people were born with severe Iodine Deficiency Disorders including brain damage. One study measured the average IQ of children in Tibet as 85, compared to an expected average of 100.

There was a salt factory in Tibet's capital, Lhasa, that produced iodised salt, but Cres suspected this salt wasn't reaching the people of Tibet.

Cres and his team visited Tibetan villages to do random checks on salt.

'This is the house,' said Mu Li, pointing to one doorway in a row of stone houses. A black fluffy dog was tied up nearby and barked as they came closer.

The house had a low doorway decorated above with coloured tiles. Cres stepped into the house with the rest of the group following. He was accompanied by other researchers, a Tibetan translator and Chinese guides and officials.

Cres greeted the homeowner, who was an older woman with a smile that made her whole face crinkle with a thousand folds. Through a translator, Cres asked what salt the woman owned. She brought out a white bag, with blue writing and a logo that said the salt was iodised. This was the only salt that could be legally sold for humans in China, including Tibet. It was the good salt.

Cres was pleased, but the house also had other salt in a blue container. Cres picked up a little salt and poured a starch solution onto the crystals. If the salt contained iodine, it would turn black. It was the same reaction he'd used in the vitamin C chemistry experiment at school.

He looked at the pink salt crystals in his hands. Their colour hadn't changed. The salt wasn't iodised.

Cres wanted to understand why the woman had good and bad salt in her house. Through a translator he asked how much she paid for the salt. She explained that the iodised salt was one and a half times more expensive. In a place where people had barely enough money to survive, it wasn't surprising that they chose the cheaper option.

He thanked the woman before he left. He was grateful that she'd welcomed him into her home and answered his questions. Cres needed to gain the community's trust, or he'd never be able to help.

Banning salt without iodine had worked well in most of China, but Cres understood it was harder in Tibet. Harvesting salt from lakes had been part of Tibetan culture for centuries. And it was usually used in barter trading for other goods. If the salt trade was banned, many families would face extreme poverty.

It would take a long time to change and in the meantime another generation of children would suffer the consequences of iodine deficiency.

Cres believed that a person's most basic human right was to use the intelligence that they'd inherited from their parents. Iodine deficiency robbed people of this right. Cres felt lucky he'd been able to develop his skills and knowledge through education. It had allowed him to have a full life and help other people. He wanted this opportunity for everyone.

Seeing the continuing problems in Tibet was a dark moment for Cres. He wondered if his work would be for nothing. Maybe the time spent away from his home and family was meaningless.

This happened to Cres sometimes. He would feel discouraged and hopeless. But he never stayed that way, he knew that wouldn't help anyone. He needed to find solutions.

So, Cres and Mu Li developed a plan to prevent brain damage in Tibetan babies and children. This plan took into account the specific circumstances in Tibet. It received funding from the Australian government and the World Health Organisation.

The plan included a program to give iodised oil capsules to Tibetan children under two years old and women of child-bearing age. One capsule contained enough iodine for a whole year. It wasn't a permanent solution, but it would prevent brain injuries in the short-term, giving the salt industry time to change.

Tibetan Buddhism is the dominant religion in Tibet. It is very important to many Tibetans and monks are highly respected. Cres knew if monks recommended something, people would listen. So the team explained the benefit of iodine capsules to Tibetan monks who then helped convince people to take the capsules.

As a result, iodised oil capsules reached an amazing 95% of the target groups of women and children. This protected around 20,000 babies each year.

In the meantime, the team tried to increase production of iodised salt in Tibet. As Mu Li spoke Mandarin and also understood the science and culture, she coordinated this program. Iodised salt from the factory in Lhasa was sent to licensed salt sellers. If you didn't have a licence, you weren't allowed to sell salt. Sellers had to keep a record of

salt delivery and sales, and these were checked by the authorities.

To increase demand for iodised salt, the project included an education program. Videos, radio programs and posters were made to spread the message about the importance of iodine and iodised salt.

The project also trained people in Tibet on how to prevent Iodine Deficiency Disorders. This meant the work would continue when Cres and his team were no longer involved. Cres's aim was to no longer be needed.

At this time, Cres was head of the Institute of Clinical Pathology and Medical Research at Westmead Hospital, which was more than a full-time job. But rather than using his annual leave to have a relaxing holiday, Cres would often go on arduous trips to remote Tibetan villages.

While there, he needed to wear an oxygen mask every evening and still felt the effects of high altitude and his previous illness in Tibet. This worried his family, but he was determined to make people's lives better wherever he could.

Cres didn't let obstacles stop him. There were lots of them: confusing officials and rules, different cultures, difficult terrain and dangerous conditions. It would have been easy to say, 'It's too hard.' But Cres didn't.

The results were wonderful. The number of Tibetan children with goitres fell dramatically. More importantly, Tibetan children stopped being born with brain injuries caused by iodine deficiency. It's estimated that the program raised the IQ of Tibetan children by 10 points. This meant they could get a better education, which would help them deal with challenges and get better jobs.

In 2003 an Australian filmmaker named, Kate Riedl, made a documentary about Cres's work titled, 'The Man Who Saved a Million Brains'. Cres was a little embarrassed by the title. He'd only agreed to the documentary to raise awareness of the importance of iodine—he didn't want it to be all about him.

But the title was also accurate. Cres's unwillingness to give up or to ignore other people's suffering meant that millions of people in Tibet and China as well as other countries were saved from brain injuries.

12

Australia

Cres sat at his desk looking at the latest survey results from 2002. The numbers were a shock. Children in Sydney weren't getting enough iodine. There were similar findings in Melbourne and Tasmania. In the past few years Cres had also noticed more people coming to his clinic with goitres. It looked as if iodine deficiency was becoming a problem in Australia again.

Europeans who had visited and then colonised Australia didn't write about Aboriginal people having goitres. This suggests that Australia's First Peoples' diets contained enough iodine. For people living on the coast this would have come from plants grown in iodine rich soils and seafood. People living inland may have got iodine from underground water supplies or by eating the thyroid glands of other animals.

By the 20th century though, lots of people in Australia had goitres and were iodine deficient. That changed again in the 1950s when dairy farmers started using iodine as a disinfectant. However, by the 21st century, it appeared that iodine deficiency in Australia was back. So, what had changed this time?

In the 1990s, the dairy industry stopped using iodine as a disinfectant and switched to chlorine-based products, so the concentration of iodine in milk dropped dramatically.

Cres had helped countries like China, Malaysia, Laos, Vietnam, Cambodia and Thailand with this issue. He was very disturbed that now it was happening in his home country. Cres knew he would have to come up with a plan.

*

That weekend, Cres was at the supermarket with Annette. Their four children were coming home for a family dinner and they wanted it to be special.

Cres walked down an aisle pushing a trolley.

'Do you think pav for dessert?' asked Annette.

'Sounds good.'

He stopped in front of the salt. There were rows of salt packets. Pink salt, river salt, sea salt flakes. None of these contained iodine. On the shelf below sat the good salt, the iodised salt. These packets were much harder to see. No wonder people kept buying the trendy, un-iodised salts.

Annette kept walking as Cres got to work rearranging the salt packets, making sure the iodised salt was at eye level and easy to access.

'Cres!' said Annette. 'What are you doing?'

Cres straightened up.

'I'm fixing the shelves,' he said.

'What's wrong with them?'

'Only 10% of Australian households have iodised salt. It's because there's this terrible stuff around.' Cres gestured at the gourmet salts, now on the lowest shelf towards the back.

'Have you been moving the salt again?' asked Annette.

Cres nodded proudly.

'That is *so* embarrassing!' whispered Annette.

Cres replied, 'Not as embarrassing as a wealthy country like Australia having iodine deficiency!'

A woman came and stood beside Cres, examining the products. She picked up a packet of iodised salt. Cres grinned. He was hoping to make much bigger changes in Australia, but stealthy supermarket shelf arranging was satisfying too.

*

In 2003 Cres and the Westmead team began the National Iodine Nutrition Study. The study aimed to find out how much iodine deficiency there was in Australia. Cres was the project's director and Mu Li the project manager. They were also supported by doctors and scientists in the states they visited.

A **random sample** of children were selected for the study. Their iodine levels would be measured by taking urine samples because 90% of iodine consumed comes straight out in urine. So, by

A **random sample** is a subsection of the population chosen at random. This means each member of the population has an equal chance of being picked.

measuring the concentration of iodine in a child's urine, researchers could tell how much iodine they had been consuming.

As well as providing a urine sample, the children's thyroid glands would be measured using ultrasound. To ensure parents would agree to the research, the team needed to make it as easy as possible, so the researchers had to go to them.

A special vehicle, known as the ThyroMobile, was brought over from Germany. It contained all the equipment they needed for the tests. The only thing it didn't have was air-conditioning!

The team hit the road. Over two years the National Iodine Nutrition Study covered 27,000 kilometres, visiting schools across Australia. This is further than driving all around the coast of Australia. The schools were randomly selected, and the tests were only carried out with permission from children's parents. Cres and Mu Li travelled to Western Australia, New South Wales, Queensland and South Australia.

At the end of each school visit, Cres gave certificates to the students, thanking them for taking part. Cres personally wrote out each student's name carefully in black ink. Unlike many doctors, Cres has good handwriting—the nuns at Woodburn had made sure of that. Cres always made time for small things like this. It meant people knew he valued their help.

The National Iodine Nutrition Study showed that half of Australian children weren't getting enough iodine. According to the World Health Organisation's standards Australia was now rated as an iodine-deficient nation.

Children need 120 micrograms of iodine each day and adults need 150 micrograms. Pregnant people need almost twice that amount: 250

micrograms each day. Clearly, many Australians weren't getting this from their diets.

Cres had a lot of experience convincing foreign governments to change their policies. Now he needed to ask his own government for change. It was a frustrating process. Australia could make iodised salt compulsory by law, like China had. This would immediately solve the problem of Australians not getting enough iodine.

However, in Australia big food companies made arguments about the rights of people to choose what they buy.

In the end, a compromise was reached. In 2009 it became mandatory to use iodised salt in bread and bread products for sale in Australia and New Zealand.

The new rules for bread were effective and raised iodine levels enough for most Australians. But iodine deficiency is still a problem in some remote areas and pregnant people in Australia need to take supplements to ensure they get enough iodine.

*

In 2020, Cres was walking with Annette around Sydney Harbour. He'd had a busy week as usual, seeing patients and meeting with students. On their walk he told Annette details about his latest project, a study on iodine deficiency in pregnancy in the Northern Territory.

They bought takeaway coffees and were walking down steep stone steps, admiring the view of the Sydney Harbour Bridge and the Opera House. Cres remembered coming to this spot on his trips home from boarding school, before the Opera House was built. It was hard for him to remember how the harbour had looked back then.

It wasn't just the view that had changed. It now seemed amazing to Cres that as a 13-year-old boy he'd been allowed to roam around Sydney by himself for the day before catching the train to Lismore alone. He was sure his grandchildren didn't have as much freedom.

Suddenly, he felt his left foot slip and then saw his coffee cup fly into the air.

The next thing he saw was a ceiling. His vision was blurry, but he could make out a railing above him, and recognised hospital curtains. He didn't usually see them from this angle though. He was lying down and someone was holding his hand.

He looked over and saw Annette sitting in the chair beside his bed. She smiled.

Then he heard the swish of curtains being drawn back and saw a young doctor come and stand over him.

'Professor Eastman,' said the man.

'Hello,' said Cres. He was confused about what had happened.

'You've had an accident. You hit your head when you fell on the steps. We also think you may have injured your hand.'

'Of course,' said Cres. It made sense, he had a splitting headache, and his hand hurt.

'I need to ask you some questions,' said the doctor.

'Fine, fine,' said Cres.

The doctor began asking questions and Cres recognised the procedure as testing for concussion. He'd done the same thing many times himself.

After the tests the man said to him, 'Do you know who I am?'

Cres was confused and replied, 'You're a doctor?'

The man laughed.

'Yes, but I was your student at Westmead two years ago.'

Recognition flooded back to Cres.

'Of course, I remember you,' he said, feeling slightly embarrassed. He was usually extremely good at remembering not only people's names, but conversations, and details about their lives.

'To be honest,' said the doctor, 'it's a bit nerve-wracking treating one of my professors!'

'I'm sure you're doing well,' said Annette reassuringly.

It took Cres some time to recover from his accident. Like many people, Cres spent 2020 working from home. He didn't see patients but was busy reviewing scientific papers, writing book chapters, and supervising research projects.

One day he received a letter from a woman he'd known when he worked in Canberra. Her daughter was born in the Canberra Hospital just after Cres introduced thyroid hormone tests for newborns—the test Cres and Jo Corcoran had developed together.

In the letter, the woman explained that the test had picked up a thyroid issue in her newborn daughter, who had then been successfully treated. Without this medication, the girl would have experienced a brain injury and growth delays due to lack of thyroid hormones. The woman told Cres that her daughter was now grown up and had completed a science degree, represented Australia in rowing and had a successful career. She reminded Cres that some people had opposed the new test and wrote, 'Thank God, you never gave up'.

Cres helped many people directly as a doctor and inspired many students in their medical careers. But there are also many people who Cres has helped who don't even know. By never giving up on his mission to prevent iodine deficiency, Cres has stopped problems from existing in the first place.

He has been involved in projects in many countries including China, Malaysia, Indonesia, Cambodia, Thailand, East Timor, and Australia. His projects have been extremely successful and led to a reduction in goitres and brain damage caused by a lack of iodine.

The World Health Organisation has said the eradication of Iodine Deficiency Disorders is equal in importance to ridding the world of smallpox. However, with iodine deficiency, the job is never done. As long as humans live in areas that don't naturally have enough iodine, efforts are needed to make sure people get iodine in another way.

Cres's scientific research helped explain why and how iodine impacts on people's health and then he went about finding solutions. These solutions improved the lives of millions of people.

Cres appreciates the opportunities and experiences he has had during his career as a clinical scientist. He's travelled the world, learned about things that fascinate him and become a pilot. The world opened up to him in a way he never imagined as a boy in Evans Head, or when he was a sheltered teenager at boarding school.

Cres has saved millions of brains. He is grateful for the opportunity to help people through his medical career. 'Medicine doesn't owe me anything,' he always says. 'I owe medicine a lot.'

Glossary

- **Aerodrome:** An aerodrome is an area of land used for the arrival and departure of aircraft.
- **Anaesthetic:** An anaesthetic is a substance that stops pain. A general anaesthetic makes a person unconsciousness and free of pain.
- **Antibiotics:** Medicine used to treat illnesses or infections caused by tiny organisms called bacteria. Antibiotics work by killing the bacteria or preventing them from multiplying.
- **Clinical:** Relating to medical observation and treatment of real patients.
- **Concentration:** A measure of how much of a substance is mixed in with another substance.
- **Diethyl ether:** A clear liquid chemical with a sweet smell. It was used as an anaesthetic in surgery. Often just called 'ether'.
- **Endocrinology:** A medical speciality treating people with conditions caused by problems with hormones such as diabetes and thyroid disorders.
- **Goitre:** A swelling in the thyroid gland in the neck.
- **Hormones:** Chemicals that tell cells and body parts to do certain things. They are made in one part of the body and travel to other parts of the body.

- **Iodine:** A chemical element. Humans need a small amount of iodine to stay healthy. Also, iodine solution can be used as a disinfectant to kill germs.
- **Iodine deficiency:** Not getting enough iodine for normal thyroid gland function.
- **Iodine Deficiency Disorders:** A range of medical problems caused by not getting enough iodine.
- **IQ:** Stands for Intelligence Quotient. This is a score that comes from a set of standardised tests that aim to measure a person's intelligence.
- **Mandatory:** Something that must be done according to a rule or law. There may be punishments or fines if it isn't done.
- **Thyroid:** An organ located in the neck and shaped like a butterfly. It makes hormones needed by all cells in the body. Thyroid hormones control how fast the body uses energy and how children grow.

About Penny Tangey

Penny Tangey writes humorous books for young people. Her most recent book, *As Fast As I Can*, won The Griffith University Children's Book Award at the 2020 Queensland Literary Awards and the Readings Children's Book Prize 2021.

Penny studied arts/science at Melbourne University, majoring in chemistry and Indonesian.

While at university, Penny performed stand-up comedy, including in the Melbourne Comedy Festival. Penny works as a researcher for television quiz shows *Hard Quiz* and *The Chase*, but she's still terrible at trivia. She is studying information management to become a librarian.